Re
Lou

A
Reason to
Love Them

Breaking the chains of trauma.

Daniela Svampa Cowie

YouCaxton Publications
Oxford & Shrewsbury

ISBN 978-1-913425-12-8
Published by YouCaxton Publications 2019
YCBN: 01

YouCaxton Publications
enquiries@youcaxton. co. uk

Disclaimer
I have conveyed the events used as examples in this book from
my memories and perception of them. In order to maintain their
anonymity, in some instances, for both legal and safety purposes,
I have changed the names of certain individuals. The change of
names is in line with my first book to ensure continuity and give the
reader a point of reference.

Contents

Looking back through the eyes of hindsight,
now that wounds have been licked
and mostly healed;
compassion, understanding and a greater
kind of love reigns.
A bigger picture, a clearer insight emerges,
on how the links,
the puzzle pieces that create
the masterpiece and connects us all,
beautifully come together.
Through our chosen vision of either pain,
joy or both... we grow.

With love

Daniela

Foreword

I would like to formally introduce myself to those of you who have not journeyed with me with my first book. My name is Daniela, I am an integrative therapy counsellor, and following the publication of 'A Reason to Love Me' my life story, I am now also an author and speaker.

This book is different than my previous one, whilst my previous writing was a recount of my life experiences and all of its trial and tribulations, here I am sharing perspectives which have helped me heal and find my peace. Offering opinions, views, and posing you questions which are aimed to provoke thought with the hope to help you find yours. What qualifies me to write this book you may ask, after all I am not a professor, I don't have a PhD, not even a degree. As paper acclaims go, what I do have several High-Level Diplomas in counselling psychotherapy and hypnotherapy.

What does qualify me in my opinion however, and is high on my scale of priorities, is that I do have a lifetime of mind-blowing experiences from which I have come back from; some of which have almost robbed me of my life. I also have, under my belt, over a decade and a half of successfully helping people find themselves and live the happy life they deserve, by sharing the techniques which have brought me back to life. I am a survivor of trauma who has come to believe, and has now made it her mission to share, the message that nothing is insurmountable.

Although not a recount as such, I have decided to write this book in the same footprint as my first one, maintaining a personal approach, authenticity and hopefully easy access for the reader. So again, by choice, I will not have this book officially edited either.

'A Reason To Love Them' is a follow up from my first book 'A Reason To Love Me', a heart wrenching memoir of my life where I struggle to find self-love. In this book, I am aiming to provide insights, 'how to', and point of views that have helped me to overcome those, apparently insurmountable events and become the happy woman that I am today.

The chapters in this book are in no way random. They have been titled in line with the topics raised in my autobiography. I have chosen these, not only to give a deeper insight into my life journey but also to better outline how the perspective I am offering has come to support my healing.

I have replaced the word 'Me' with 'Them' as I have come to believe that although it can be incredibly hard to find self-love at times, it can be just as hard, learning to love 'Them' and freeing ourselves. By 'Them' I mean anyone that we feel have done us wrong, hurt us, belittled us, caused us physical and/ or emotional pain. Anyone that we believe has left a scar (or two), on our body, heart and soul.

We all at some point or another in our lives, go out of our way to impress, fit in or try to be liked or loved by others; our parents, a potential lover, a social group or even ourselves. In my case, all of the above; from childhood through the different stages in my life. All the time checking, copying, following, 'reading' someone else, whether the leader of a pack (my dad), or the pretty girl, or the clever guy... Always wearing different masks in order to be in the 'in' crowd, to be accepted, liked or loved. It is by playing this 'game' that we often lose ourselves, that we forget our worth and who we truly are. In so doing we give away our power. Some people will notice what we are doing and give it right back, praising us, reminding us of our strengths and qualities, of our uniqueness; most people however won't. If we dare to delve deeper, we can come to realize that these people are not mean, they are not evil, in fact if we look beyond the surface, we are able to see that they too are fighting a battle. A battle we know nothing about... they too are learning in the only way they know how.

It is my opinion that no one is born 'bad' and hopefully through the lines of my writing I will be able to substantiate and give credit to this point. On one account, I believe we might be born with health deficiencies, neurological disorders and serious mental health conditions which would cause us to behave in a certain manner if these are not addressed and controlled. Another aspect to consider is, we might have learnt unhealthy views and behaviours from our surroundings, so in turn develop certain beliefs, no doubt some more radical than others, some even to indoctrination level, which again would bring about choices and behaviours which can damage others; but nobody is born 'bad'.

Perpetrators do not behave the way they do just for the sake of doing so. They too, although perhaps at times with many detrimental actions and results through their general daily deeds, come, like the rest of us mortal, from a place of fear, pain, ignorance or illness.

I believe everyone is walking a path which creates different designs in this huge tapestry called life. Imagine a huge canvas where with each action we take, we make a stitch and as the stitches amount, they create pictures, the events in our lives. Every time we come into contact with one another, together we create a stitch that gives that image character, colour, shape, purpose even; touching and shaping both lives, leaving an imprint, which each individual uses to learn and grow from their own unique perspective. Every stitch, every encounter every image carries a lesson that helps to create the bigger picture of this huge puzzle of life. An image which we get to make sense of, we get to understand the further along we go. Everything, everyone has a purpose; no one comes empty handed.

With this book I look to offer a different perspective other than the one that seems to be our default setting, the one that, based on fear, causes us to react with negative emotions and feelings. The 'go to' setting generally is one of judgement, anger, resentment, hate, disgust and so on... All negative feelings and emotions that harm US, the people who feel these feelings, not the perpetrators. All I am asking for is for you to keep an open mind, as it's thanks to this precious attitude, my willingness to try, through trial and error that I have come to heal, find peace and overcome the upheaval in my life.

I have written each chapter with a specific purpose in mind; not to excuse the perpetrators but to free you from the addiction of self-loathing, self-sabotaging, rescuing, pointing fingers and 'victim mode'. We often go through life unconnected, playing catchup, aloof, lost even; not only unaware we have chosen this course, but that we have the power to change it by simply altering our perspective. Through each chapter under various scenarios, I offer a different view, a more healing view, a view which, rather than focussing on pain, victimhood and blame, focuses on compassion, self-empowerment, growth and taking responsibility for our own lives, and seeking solutions. The aim here is to create thought-provoking images, and help you take your power back; to encourage you to live life on your terms, in happiness and joy. Although some chapters could be expanded vastly, in this book I will limit them to provide only a few points so to give an idea and help address the thoughts I try to stimulate without overburdening or complicating matters.

I am sure those of you who have read my life story are probably eager to know how I could even consider applying the word love to the man who almost took my life away. I have intentionally left that particular trauma to the end as I hope to gradually introduce you to the mindset that will help you to better understand, or if not at least appreciate, the belief and power that supported, and still supports me in keeping love and peace in my heart, for all.

Some points may be repeated throughout this book, not as a mistake or as a means of filling the pages, but because I believe them to be important in the purpose of driving home the point I seek to make. You may also find that some of the points and descriptions I use in a chapter may also apply to others; this is because the subject matter not only runs parallel together but often intertwines.

Chapter One

If I Knew Then What I Know Now

Hindsight is a wonderful thing if it is used as a tool to learn, to develop and to better one's life. Used to look back, summarise and deduce, grasp the lessons and confidently apply them to current situations, will make us a bunch of very emotionally healthy, well balanced, beautifully growing human beings. However, this is rarely the approach most of us take. The approach that most of us tend to take consciously or unconsciously when using the gift of hindsight is very different; we take hindsight, and we use it to beat ourselves up… repeatedly.

All of us want to be 'know it all's', always getting it right; none of us want to make mistakes, gosh they are so embarrassing! And then there is that thing, 'Failure' God forbid we should fit under that umbrella and show ourselves as one of those people that are labelled as failures! It would be the end of the world as we know it. I see it every day, with my children, with my children's friends, I have seen it over the years when I worked in a school environment, I see it in my therapy sessions with my clients, that are getting younger and younger. The fear of getting it wrong, the fear of rejection, the fear of other people's opinion, the fear of been ridiculed, judged and cast aside. The need to be included is laced with the fear of exclusion. Not a thought is spared to how much venom we swallow as we turn the fight inward, killing our self-love and self-acceptance. We don't see how much damage we do to ourselves by being so dependent on the words, opinions and ways of others who, at the end of the day like ourselves, are living by the seat of their pants, basing our decisions on simple 'guess work'. We disregard our beautiful gift of being unique.

I am the first one to admit, I used to feel ashamed of being different. Very ashamed. I envisioned me as a leper, a reject, a sprout of the dark force, a nullity. . Now, with experiences under my belt, hindsight, and an avalanche of emotional scars earned through some bumpy life lessons, my view is somewhat changed. Now all I feel is pride, authenticity and uniqueness. I envision me as a shade of the most beautiful undiscovered colour, and it is my purpose to make it known. Some of you might think this as big headed, but if you have read my book 'A Reason to Love Me' you will know that, this could not be further away from an accurate description of me. The truth is I extend this vision to every other living soul. Far from being big headed, I have actually learned to finally raise myself to the same level as everyone else; what differs from my original feelings is that I am now on a par, an equal playing field. Through this vision, through this approach, I can see beauty and individuality in everyone, and this frees me of judgement toward them (and most of the time towards me) and helps me see through the eyes of love and acceptance.

Love is a powerful thing, we all want it, forgetting that we all have it! It seems to be common practice that from the moment we are born, this very natural emotion that we embody when we come into this world, gets hammered and drained out of us. We are 'sold' this idea that it is selfish to have love for oneself, that in order to be complete we need others to love us. The message we often get is that to be loved is the be all and end all, that we are nothing without another's love. This message deepens when we proceed to attach different meanings to this beautiful sentiment and love starts to become acceptance, importance, worth, compliance, obedience and so on. Although all of these can be an expression of love, they are not love. Love is love. It is a feeling, a sentiment in its own right; love just is. Unfortunately, often, not through ill intention but more through emotional ignorance, we can manipulate or let ourselves be manipulated under the name of love: - "If you loved me you would/wouldn't do this" or "If you weren't so this or that, it would be easier to love you" or even "If you kept your opinions to yourself, people would like you more". And it is so that with each attachment and each statement passed down from the very people we trust and love, we step away from our true source, from our inner love, the unconditional love which includes unconditional love for ourselves. As these messages add up day after day into our subconscious, the tank of inner love empties and begins to fill with doubts, confusion and a need for outer validation.

So, with time we strip ourselves of the power that we are. We forget our worth, our uniqueness, our attributes, our amazing resources; we reject those parts of ourselves to fit in. Unaware and cheated, we sell out for a handful of promises that the outside world will deliver a love which will make us happy and complete. I too, once a young spirited girl, filled with enough of the above messages, bought into this belief and endured years of severe upset and turmoil.

As a young child, I was full of questions and opinions, always challenging what did not ring true to me. I would argue my point, I would give my reasons, I would tell the truth when asked a question regardless if it was not what the person wanted to hear, or not to the liking of bystanders that simply held a different opinion. I defended others that I felt were victimised or unfairly treated; I always tried to be true and fair to all (the truth and fairness as I saw it in each moment). To me this was 'me', my natural character, how I aligned and understood life. Soon however, I was to be moulded into a different 'me', because this one, I was brought to believe, wasn't good enough. The natural me apparently did not fit in with the family ways, their social reflection or the community expectations. So, the programming messages began to flow, some directly some underhandedly… "What are people going to say?!", "You need to be more humble", "Don't be so selfish!", "You are just a child what could you possibly know", "No one asked for your opinion, this is nothing to do with you!", "Go to confession and say sorry for arguing back!", or generally being made a laughing stock of, by simply being shamed and ridiculed. With a strong inner sense of right and wrong, at first I fought for me, for the right to be me, but with repetition, punishments and general ways of 'I am going to make your world hell', unable to find a way out, I finally broke, capitulated and moulded to fit into this mask they all wanted me to wear.

Looking back, knowing what that change, that 'selling out' meant to me and for me, would I have been able to do anything different? Would I have done anything different? Possibly not. As every step that girl took, every choice she has made, has made me the person who I have become and who I am happy in being. Without even one of those lessons, those feelings and emotions, I would not have come to view myself, the world or life exactly as I view them now. You often hear the question, "what would you tell your younger self?" With <u>my</u> hindsight, if I could speak to the young me, I would use my words to reassure her, to tell her that one day someone will understand her, **I** will understand her, that one day **I** will love her. I would tell her that I get her, I understand each and every choice she has made and that they are all accounted for, none of them wasted; she has no blame to carry. I would tell her that I know that she made the best of what she had, with the surroundings, circumstances, people and scenarios she found herself in.

I would tell her "I love you, and I am sorry for the pain that you have to endure now; and in many of the years that follow. I am sorry you have had to be broken in order to survive. I am sorry that you have had to forget, to cast aside, the power that you in your heart already know you are, in order to fit in and receive what crumb of love has been given in exchange". I would say to her "Thank you. Thank you for sticking with it; for although you do not know it now, although it is and will be very dark at times and the light and peace seeming so farfetched, you will persevere and fight your way through so that I can come to be". I would say "Thank you for paying attention, as along the way when life revealed to you the hidden purpose of each challenge you faced, you collected those gems; our reward, one of immense happiness, great inner knowing, and a very profound sense of self-love". I would tell her "You are beautiful and amazing; despite the outer input and your young perception, there is nothing wrong with you! This journey, these experiences are just part of your growth; lessons needed for you to comprehend and appreciate yourself as a whole, to understand where you fit in this world and which part you have come to play. Lessons, that are going to prepare you and set you in line with your life purpose; for through these you will discover more of yourself, of your strength, and learn the skills to make a better difference to the world in the future". I would tell her "Don't fight yourself so hard; have more trust in your inner knowing and don't worry so much; everything passes". If I could sneak her a 'tantum of hope' I would tell her "Perspective is a gift, if you change the way you see your world you will see more of the gems and less of the pain, in each situation and path you walk; gems that will bring you home to your original self, the 'you' that was uncontaminated by judgement and social expectations". I would tell her "I love you unconditionally, so live, be, explore, test, and hold your head up high whenever you can. I am proud of you and all that you are; and although they might force a behaviour change, they cannot change the spirit of a strong mind and the will of a loving heart... it will always find its way home to source."

I would tell her, "I know all this, because I've got you now"

To keep the younger me strong and focussed whilst flying under their radar, I would teach her a new game, the 'Good Opposites' game. A game that would help retain all her inner qualities strong and present, a game, where balance is kept. The rules of the game? 'For every negative word or sentence they throw your way, search within your mind and tell yourself the exact opposite'. Be sure to match any amount of negativity with the same amount (and more!), of positivity.

Finally, I would tell her that although the loneliness she felt was overbearing she was never alone, as inside her resides all the company she could muster if she only acknowledged herself and looked within. For all those times she felt unloved, it would reveal the masked truth, that all those adults hid behind… they did indeed love her, they just did not know how to show it or how to lead with that love. They did their best with what they knew and although that best was damaging to her, that is all they had to offer.

<u>A reason to love them</u> - These people, the people that were shaping me into their view of how I should be, were not children. In fact, I never did come across a child in my childhood that behaved in such a damaging manner toward me. These people were adults, they were the adults I was dependent on, my parents, the nuns in the convent school I was sent to, to improve me. But, were they bad people? Were they out to get me? Did they hate me? No, they didn't. Their behaviour was a simple reflection of their feelings toward themselves, of their view on life and its rules. They were simply acting on their own knowledge and perspective on 'correct' living, teaching and raising children. They behaved in accordance to their own learnt lessons and acquired beliefs. They just followed what they knew, and in my parents and carers case, leading by power, aggression, oppression and anything that stopped anyone from questioning them, their knowledge, actions and their feelings. Living by anything that would cover up their fears of showing their vulnerabilities and the fact that, like most of us, being new to each life experience, they were just 'winging it'.

Through my life experiences and my own lessons, as I hinted in the Foreword, I have come to believe (however controversial this might be), that when people behave in an unkind, damaging manner, it is not because they were born bad or are evil, they do so out of ignorance, fear, indoctrination or illness. So, with this in mind, how can we place blame on, or hate someone, that simply does not know any better? Don't get me wrong with this I don't mean that we excuse them or condone their behaviour, stay trapped and suck it up, no; we can understand and accept, but we do not have to oblige, endure or enable their behaviour. Although this might not apply to a child as when we are young restrictions are inevitable, options are more limited, and the 'Good Opposites' game might be more useful in certain situations, and telling the relevant authorities in others; as adults we have more choices available to us. For a start, we can love them, and we can still leave them, as it is okay for us to shed the people that no longer fit our ways or growth in a healthy manner. An issue we might encounter in doing so here is stepping away without holding guilt's hand. Guilt is often a concept taught to us by those very people who wanted us to live life from their perspective only and follow their rules for life. Through that guilt we tend to feed the message that we are not a good person for leaving people behind, regardless of how detrimental they may be to our emotional wellbeing. Guilt can also be at the base of adopting a self-defence mechanism whereby we go on the defence and point the blaming fingers, thus directing our focus to fault and misplaced responsibilities.

When making decisions we can only work from the standpoint of what we have come to know at each given moment and situation, and act upon that knowing. With this acknowledgement it does not serve us to judge our past actions. Although we might have chosen to enable or entertain behaviours which did not serve us, and even lose ourselves in the process in order to please whatever inner belief we had come to own, at the moment we have a shift in need, it's okay for us to make a different decision. As Maya Angelou said, "Do the best you can until you know better. Then when you know better do better". We do not have to leave our peaceful state in order to make changes in our lives, that only occurs when we become reactive to that person or situation or we cross the boundaries of responsibilities. It helps to bring in 'check points', asking ourselves how we really feel about that person, situation or behaviour and even, whether they serve us and our growth. As soon as we learn that their behaviour does not serve us, as soon as we find ourselves living less than a worthy life, as soon as we find a safe way, we can then take back our power and we make different, better choices. Whether these choices are to go, learn a new way, or stand our ground, it is important to empower ourselves toward any person or situation that makes us feel less than ourselves. It is important to take our own responsibility for our part, our ability to shape the direction of OUR lives; leaving them with their own responsibility over theirs, their path, their growth. The real trick here, yet the most rewarding one, really is resisting the temptation to hold on to the anger and the need to place blame. This would only serve to keep US stuck, viewing ourselves as powerless victims, thus hurting ourselves, not them. Keep practicing the act of bringing your attention back to you, to your life; to what you have an influence over and can change.

Just a little extra tip here to reiterate and reinforce the point for those who like me struggle with guilt. Remember that by distancing ourselves, by speaking up or by taking back our power, we are not being bad, rejecting them or judging them; we can still love them and accept them at their core, soul and human level; we just don't love, accept or choose to entertain their behaviour anymore. We simply choose not to succumb to their victimising traits any longer. Every time we justify, we keep them and ourselves stuck in a repetitive pattern; as we behave in accordance with what is true to ourselves, our worth and needs, we create different outcomes, promote growth and lessons learnt, for the benefit of all concerned.

Chapter Two

Abandonment and Rejection

The dictionary definition of abandonment is 'To leave a place, thing, or person, usually for ever'. Short sweet and to the point. However, if we dig deeper, abandonment is much more than just that, than just an action, a change of location. It is also a feeling, an emotion, a pain, a rejection, a trauma, a place from which most of us spend a great part of our life trying to come back from. It is not only the ones that are left in orphanages, or those that have been given up for adoption, or even those that have lost a parent or have had a parent moving out that feel the pinch of abandonment. In my case, although I had no idea in my younger years, I was suffering from a case of just that, abandonment. I too felt these very emotions and yet none of the situations listed applied to me. Granted, I did not place a label on it, but I did feel its grip, I felt in my own unique way, abandoned. Those times when as a little girl, I kept been sent away, whether it was to some relative's house or the convent boarding school, where I felt my parents barely gave me the time of day for a visit and kept me there for six years. A place where I felt my sense of insignificance was sealed, every time they did come and visit and they spent most of their time giving their attention to the nuns or the other girls. All those times that I was shamed, unreasonably punished, those times when I hurt myself and asked for nothing more than reassurance I was scolded, insulted, shouted at and sent away… that to me was abandonment, that to me was rejection. When I think of the loneliness, the rejection, the feeling of generally being unwanted, that feeling that abandonment brought, one time in particular comes to mind, one time above all others… Whilst in the convent school I was allocated an American family to write to as my 'adoptive' family. The nuns demanded I kept in contact with these people despite me reminding them that I did have a mum and dad, that although these people were very lovely people, I already had a family. When I told my parents of this, no reassuring response was offered. The questions this raised in my head, I can't even begin to tell you. I just don't have the words.

I spent many years cementing beliefs of inadequacy, of non-belonging, of not being good enough to be 'let in' anywhere… by anyone. I learned to accept and make all these emotions, messages and beliefs a part of me, reinforcing them day after day. If I did not practice them within my surroundings, by putting myself in situations where I would feel useless and undervalued, I certainly reinforced them through my own self-talk. Somewhere along the way, I learnt to reject me; I abandoned myself. Through my ignorance, my ability to recognise that I was treating myself the same way I was treated from the outside; I had joined the perpetrators in their actions against me. I allowed this seed of rejection and abandonment to leave me behind, to turn me, into my own worst enemy. Day after day feeding more and more my sense of self worthlessness, my insecurities and low self-belief, belittling myself at any given opportunity, then and for years to come, I re-created in my relationships that feeling of rejection. This repetition, although excruciating as it was to experience, was what I'd grown to know, thus, it felt like 'home'. By the time I reached adulthood my worthlessness was so ingrained that I only attracted people whose need to feel empowered needed to be fuelled, people that would only be too happy to keep me under their thumb, foot, heel… you name it. What I did not realize was that I was the one that had placed me there. Relationships so destructive where I could (although consciously unaware), play the 'victim' role, allowing me to feel alone, left to fight my inner battles as well as any outer challenging experience, alone. Relationships where, what I knew as rejection, was to be dished out to me daily.

With insight and lessons learnt, I can now see the pattern, the part I played in each relationship in my life with regards to feelings of rejection and abandonment. Beginning from my father and my desperate need to please him all the way through marrying a deluded, paranoid, psychotic man who I stood by, living in fear of, a man who with his behaviour kept alive all my inner demons. Most importantly however I have learnt that the most damaging of them all, the person that had done the most damage and inflicted the worse type of rejection on me, was in fact, me. Every time I shut myself out, every time I sided with, and justified, others' actions (well-intentioned or otherwise) at my expense... every time I had left myself behind. I was the one that was dishing out to myself the worst, most powerful and damaging kind of rejection and abandonment there is... self-rejection and self-abandonment.

It feels like it has taken me forever to 'get it', to understand this lesson, but the important thing is that 'I have got it'. Even though at times I still have words with myself for judging myself through my inner talk, where I still at times tell myself that it took me too long, that I am obviously hard of hearing... Overall, I do tend to remember that the time I needed to learn the lesson was exactly the time it was meant to take; that abandonment and rejection are a much bigger experience than the short and to the point description a dictionary can offer. I have learnt that in that time, there was more than one gem to collect along the way, more than one lesson to be learnt which made the picture and situations even bigger and the road I travelled a little more intriguing (to say the least), and a little bit longer.

<u>A reason to love them</u> - Coming from the principle that we are all here to experience life in our own unique way, from different angles and perspectives, already gives us a reason to love the people we feel have abandoned us or rejected us. They are simply fighting a different battle than the one we fight; they are simply learning a different lesson than the one we are learning, at times, opposites apart. They are seeing and experiencing that very same situation from a different angle, an angle that mirrors their own unique lessons and path.

I have now come to learn and truly believe that we are so amazingly unique, and in turn, each and everyone's path is fantastically unique. I believe that not only each one of us can and will experience the same situation in an absolute personal way, but that we will also see it and experience it from a multitude of different angles and viewpoints. With this realization, although I still instinctively react and get cross at a single event, an 'in your face' telesales caller for instance (whom I have literally just interacted with), when I step back (and have had a chance to take one or two deeper breaths!), I can see a clearer picture, I can see my lessons, their possible lessons, why the exchange took place the way it did... Did that telesales person feel rejected when, following a tirade of calls from her company over the past week, I have firmly asked her to please not call my number again? Did that make me a bad person for shutting her out of my life? I certainly did not reject her personally, but at some level, depending on her life experiences till now, she might have felt I did.

If we look deep enough into our own path, we all reject or abandon one another a lot of the time, it depends on how deep we empower our own view of rejection; what rejection means to us. A girl that loves a boy, but he does not love her back, a husband who leaves his wife because he has realised, he wants to become a monk, a child whose parents divorced and either mum or dad leaves the marital home; even those times we choose to do something different than what we are asked or disagree with someone else's point of view. The question is, are we actually rejecting or abandoning? I now personally believe not. To me, we are simply focussed on, and seeing things from our own standpoint and current knowledge; looking at it from a variety of different views…

I have come to believe that the real culprits, the real bad asses, the real abandonment and rejection to really look out for, is actually self-abandonment and self-rejection. These are the only real ones with the power to stunt our growth. They misguide us from our self-discovery, from our life mission and purpose. Still if there is a reason to love them, the outer perpetrators, there is definitely a reason to love us, our **'self-perpetrator'**, because we are the ones experiencing our life in first person, fully responsible for it. Moulding it every day with each step we take, not just learning from the outside input, but also adapting, learning and responding from the inside, via our emotions, our senses, our instincts trying to make sense of it all as we go. We are the ones dealing with the bruises we pick up when we fall during our blind guessing times having a run at a new experience; but we are also the ones that get up and brush ourselves off and keep trying till we rise.

Following is a further example that might help you to raise questions on abandonment and rejection, one which may challenge the power you may have been placing on them. Using a story that I have read somewhere as a base and expanding upon it, a story I like to remind myself and others of at those times when people for one reason or another have moved on, in this physical plane or the etherical one.

I would like you to imagine this scene: - When you are born you board a train, the train of your life. On this train there are many carriages and many doors. Throughout your life people will board your train, some will stay for a while, some will leave after a few stops, others will stay on it throughout your life journey. More and more people will board your train as your journey runs on and stay for as long as they need. Every person with their own unique path and destination. Each person will stay on your train for as long as it takes for you and them too learn the required shared lessons. Your job, your responsibility and focus throughout, is to take care of your train. To keep your train happy, welcoming, respectful and respected, loving and peaceful. To keep it free of clutter and rubbish.

Making sure that these rules are kept by all passengers. There will be times during this journey where you may have to ask someone to leave the train for not respecting your rules or meeting your needs. There will also be times however when some people, including the ones we love will leave the train of their own accord, not because they don't like your train but perhaps because it no longer meets the requirements for their needs or their destination demands a different route.

Most people don't mean to purposely or hurtfully abandon anyone; but often due to our paths, emotions, fears, feeling trapped or out of options as well as other aspects of influence, as we steer our life forward in the best way we think, at some point or another, we all leave people behind. There is always a reason behind someone's choice; principally their own needs and understanding.

Chapter Three

Eating Disorder

I started my battle with eating disorders at a very young age. As we know through countless research projects, many things can be a cause or trigger for this disorder; trauma, lack of coping skills, biology, genetics, sociocultural and so on and so forth. Many of us use food as a means to gain control, self-punish or both. When under the grip of this condition, in pain, out of control and scared, we cry out for help. A lot of people are quick to assume it's an episode of 'attention seeking' (in a loose, frowned upon way, the 'look at me way'), but this is rarely the case. People that do not suffer from this disorder cannot sustain or comprehend the diligence required to self-harm or imagine the emotional roller coaster one faces daily to beat the addiction caused by a spectrum of mental beliefs. Eating disorders are not something you can fake.

In my case, I believe it was supported by two main factors. One, an involuntary reactive body response, an automatic reaction which took place in the presence of negative experiences, or the perception of – when something unnerved me or I was upset or anxious, my stomach would knot tightly and nothing could go in, or if I did put it in it wanted to come straight out. Two, the lack of coping skills in response to emotional pain – anxiety, depression, stress and inner conflict to mention a few. A way of self-punishing and gaining control all at the same time. Although it is not easy for me to peek through the foggy layers and gather a fully clear image, as far as I can scrape together, my first battle with food was in my early years, as a result of fear and uneasiness at family conflict; in particular, anything surrounding secrets, deceit, aggressive talk, threats or malicious intent. From a very young age I struggled to understand or accept that people who loved one another would keep secrets from each other and be mean to one another. When asked to keep schtum about something, normally by my sister, I would break down, crumble and cry my eyes out until it was aired (she really hated me for it). Also, although it is quite odd, as I don't recall any 'foul play' one thing that caused me to become distressed and my stomach to clench, was having thoughts of a 'sexual' nature (or any thoughts at all regarding the opposite sex); I suppose my father threatening to kill me, my sister and my mum at any given opportunity that raised the scenario of pregnancy before marriage might have had something to do with it. I was only six years old.

Although I must admit, in addition to the two mentioned factors, there were other influences running in the background that played a part throughout the different stages in my battle with food in my life; my mother for one. Her focus on outer beauty and constant comparison to others, as well as, judgement of other people's size, didn't help. Despite being on the heavier side of her ideal weight for the majority of her adult life herself, look and dress code (highly reflective of the Italian culture I was raised in), would determine whether I was presentable to the crowd, and so be accepted by her. The culture and the local tongues where always ready to scrutinize and happily point out anything that was not quite up to scratch and for someone as sensitive as me, very insecure and with no self-worth or belief, every time that happened, they did cut deep. I remember on one occasion, Romina's grandmother (Romina was my childhood best friend), laughing at me as she saw my legs displayed whilst wearing shorts during a hot summer day, affirming that I was a 'falsa magra'; explaining that although I looked thin fully clothed in reality I had tree trunk size thighs! For someone who already had a great dislike of herself and her looks, this was a bombshell of a comment to receive. I was in awe of the women that looked stick thin, with tiny little waists and hardly any hips that I saw on tv (usually on British or American movies) and I rejected in my mind's eye any images of the curvier women. Growing up it became even more of an obsession to the point that I would hold my breath every time I saw an overweight person (as if I could 'catch' their body weight!) and breath in deeply almost to absorb the power of thinness when I saw someone with the type of figure I wanted to achieve... and the illness grew. No matter what people said, no matter how many thin or beautiful figure compliments I received throughout my life, I only saw 'disproportionate' bits in my reflection (even now I often still do).

I battled with food on and off throughout my life, in fact, I have to say it has been more on than off. Now, in spite of not being totally free of this disorder, as I always keep an eye on my weight and an overall balance of food intake, I do have a fair handle on it. However, over the years, as I said, from about age six, I have used a variety of damaging approaches to food and eating, I point blank stopped eating, refused to eat in front of people (generally boys), made myself sick, took laxatives, sought out and bought any new thing that could aid weight loss, from smelling fruit pens to ingesting tablets, tight sweaty exercise gear and pulsing machines. No matter how many times people told me I looked too thin or ill, to me I was fat, I thought I looked fat and food was the enemy I was dancing with on a regular basis.

People often find it difficult to understand and accept the realities and behaviours behind eating disorders. We often read or hear people making unfair comments about those that have issues with food. If someone is overweight, they are often accused of not having any self-discipline or being out right greedy. The person who has issues with their food intake whether they suffer from anorexia bulimia or general body dysmorphia, is wrongly accused of attention seeking and looking for compliments. I personally, have been at the receiving end of a lot of criticism, judgement and some distorted unfair accusations over my battle with this condition. Statements thrown out as if I wasn't there- "ignore her. She is just attention seeking!", "She is just after compliments", "There is something wrong with her head", all followed with the rolling of eyes or a look of disapproval or disgust; and my 'favourite'- "She is attracting attention to her body in order to pull"! This one came after I joined in a conversation where people talked about their figure and wanting to lose weight. I remember expressing my opinion of what I did not like about parts of my body which I felt and believed were holding more fat than I cared for. Whilst they supported each other's statements, I was shot down. Despite the figures and facts adding up against my logic and maybe in favour of my derisory 'friends', those comments could not have been further from the truth. I truly believed my statements, and their scornful attitude only served to make me feel more isolated, different and silly. This resulted in me embracing even more so the belief that I, my thoughts and beliefs were not adequate, important or understood and would be better left unshared; leaving me dealing with my body dysmorphia and food battle on my own.

Although with time things have improved and we are all more aware and better informed about eating disorders, it is still frowned upon and not favourably looked at especially if you are an adult. This makes it difficult for the sufferer to speak up especially if he or she has been burned by thoughtless comments and derisory sneers before.

<u>A reason to love them</u> - People who tend to judge, criticise or even try to force this disorder or perceived self-images out of those affected, normally do so because of their own uncomfortable state of mind. Over the years, I have come to observe that often fear, guilt, frustration, jealousy, insecurities and the need to control, play a strong part in people's reactions to other's life struggles, of which eating disorders are included. I have come to believe that no matter what the situation, type of interaction and behaviour, anything any of us does or says is always about ourselves, what we think, what we feel, what we believe, and so on. For example, when hitting depression at the age of six, refusing to eat and wasting away, my father at first used all the threats he could gather to force me to eat. He even tried to shove the food down my throat and eventually had the one and only melt down I have ever seen him have. Although I was the cause of his actions, the one who prompted his responses, his reactions were not really about me. They were based upon his own beliefs, his own fears, his own expectations, rules, guilt, assumptions and pride. My actions (or lack of) were possibly feeding his fear of failure. After all, for a head of a household to whom control was everything, as my father was, if his little girl was not going to get a grip, in his eyes, not only could she end up ruining his reputation but this situation would have raised questions over his own power and ability to control and lead his family. My actions had simply given him an opportunity to face *himself*, his views, his path; which, if willing to learn, would help him with his personal and interpersonal growth and development. If not, the saga would continue, and similar situations would recreate until his lesson was learnt. Would it be healthy or fair for me to pass judgement on my father when this perspective was not in his awareness? I believe my energy would be better spent on assessing my own lessons from that experience. I was faced with my very own challenges, with this interaction, as what I read into my father's way of handling my behaviour and my pain, was quite bleak and not quite as compassionate as the view I have come to hold. Taking it as a judgement and ridden with guilt I embarked on a journey of self-loathing, developing emotional and interpersonal skills based on my 'child's eye' interpretation, some of which would come to show themselves as useful and some not quite so.

As a parent now I can at times see it in my reactions to my children's actions. I on occasion must stop myself and think before I let my mouth run and jump into things which at times would just be a result of my own unresolved hang ups instead of a fair, balanced offer of direction, support and guidance. Words that would be a regurgitation from my father, mother, nuns and other powerful figures in my childhood. This proving yet again, that all that we do and say is a direct result of our own life experience, paths walked, and lessons learnt. We are always presented with choices and opportunities to grow or repeat patterns.

To use another example, not long ago, I saw a comment on Facebook where a young woman saw fit to pass judgement and cast it on social media. She was outlining how an older, overweight person should not wear leggings, as it was, in her words, 'repulsive and disgusting'. Now, this lady wearing leggings was no doubt minding her own business, going about her everyday life and certainly had not asked this young woman for validation on her clothing of choice. That day she had chosen to wear that particular item of clothing for her own reasons; maybe out of comfort, maybe because she liked the style, maybe even because in her eyes she looked good in them. Still, the young woman took it upon herself and spat out her horror at such a scene. Here I ask, was this young lady's judgement really about the older woman, her age or her size, or was it in fact about herself, her fear of how she could be perceived by those around her if she were not follow the social guide lines, the given 'standards' of how things should or should not be? Could her squabble be based on her learning of what one needs to adhere and conform to, what is acceptable in the fashion (in this case yet again, Italian) world? In her own culture and environment this young woman was taught, possibly like myself from a young age, that such decisions were unacceptable and would be judged, so in order to self-protect and fit in with the general masses, she speaks out at what seems to be the issue with another person but really it is just a reminder to the self.

On the premise that we express ourselves through our own views and perceptions, again it goes to reinforce that, none of us intentionally go out of our way to hurt. Often not having yet learnt different, more apt coping mechanisms, in order to deal with our discomfort, maybe what we see about our own figure, shape, look, eating habits, we attack those we perceive as better off and yet complain. Often people lash out simply as a method of self-preservation or on the reverse, self-sabotage by rejecting, hiding or refusing to deal with the issues that are raised within them. We often retaliate when buttons are pressed (whether intentionally or unintentionally) which raises an inner conflict, despite giving us a chance to address our inner balance and growth.

Chapter Four

Self Judgement and Self-abuse

Already from when we are young, we are taught to judge, to compare, to separate ourselves from our fellow human beings. It's not necessarily that people, namely the adults in our lives, go out of their way to teach us this lesson, they simply impart it by being living examples. As babies, toddlers, children, we copy everything, how to talk, how to walk, facial expressions, moods and so on. We listen, we watch, going back to that need for acceptance, we copy, and we learn how best to fit in; paying close attention to what works and what doesn't, what makes people happy and what does not. Learning from our surroundings we form our opinion about the world we live in and more importantly about ourselves and how we relate to it. Self-judgement comes into play when we learn to compare ourselves to others, when we measure ourselves to their behaviour, their opinion, their achievements, their life choices, to mention a few. When we feel we don't equal or surmount other's performances, when we don't come to match with what we have learnt and embodied as beliefs, as well as that which is deemed acceptable by our loved ones, our immediate support system and general society, we ask: - "Am I good enough?"

All of us in one way or another have learnt to pass judgement; whether it is about ourselves, a book, another person, someone's opinion, a home, a style or whatever. As we grow up, we develop different ways to deal with the discomfort of that judgement, specifically, self-judgement. Based on my life experiences and encounters, I have come to deduct and form a belief that the angry and fearful turn against the outside world, the sensitive and/or passive aggressive turn against their inner selves. Some of us avoid responsibilities and always look to place blame, some of us take on the world's responsibilities and place the blame within. Either way judgement comes from a place of no balance, feeling weak, vulnerable, doubting our abilities, status, likability and anything else we rate as important in the eyes of acceptance and being love worthy. Being a reflection of our point of view and beliefs, of what we have come to compute, a passing of judgement is first and foremost a dig at ourselves; questioning our worth.

I personally have fitted under the 'sensitive - passive aggressive' umbrella for most of my life. Taking on the world's responsibilities, not really expressing my thoughts or standing up for myself, always placing the blame within me. At those times when the pain caused by the inability to positively and healthily address the situations at hand, fuelling self-judgement, raised to an uncontainable level, I turned to hurt myself. All the accumulated anger would blurt out with such a force that I was unable to stop it until it had run its course. I would be my own worst enemy, my fiercest bully. Except from some of the shocking one-off, very unique sentences my mother used to conjure up to put me down, nobody else has ever been so intensely vicious or verbally abusive to me as I was to myself. I would stand in front of the mirror and would stare at myself with the most disgusted expression and hurl the most horrible, degrading, demining words I could muster; often with the addition of physical harm which in my case consisted of self-slapping, digging my nails in my skin, scratching, pulling my hair out of my head and if that was not hitting the spot head butt a wall or a door. Every attack on myself was not only to release the emotional pain by form of exchange with the physical but to punish myself for not being good enough, for not getting things right (at least the right I had come to believe to be as such by 'public expectation'). The words I would sneer to myself either through an intentional frightening whisper or shouting them were a horrid reflection of that. I hated me for not being up to par, not being good enough, not fixing the world enough, not being pretty enough... beliefs based on my own observations and understanding of the people and surroundings I lived in and the unhealthy interactions that took place; experiences that taught me to self-judge.

When we think of self-harming we immediately think of physical damage, cutting, burning oneself, overdosing etc. It is not very often that we take into consideration (unless you are in the professional mental health sector) the mental, emotional and psychological self-harm. Again, using myself as an example, the negative verbal abuse I dished out to myself during those episodes of intense pain, self-judgement and self-persecutions, were very damaging. In fact, those words would in time scar me, they'd reinforce within me, time after time, those very beliefs that caused me to hate myself, lowering my self-esteem, my self-worth and result in me living a shaky and unhappy life. The verbal self-harming with its hindering powers can be just as life arresting (coming from the perspective of the inability to live a functioning lifestyle) as the physical one. I would like to make it very clear that although here I write of self-harming on the back of self-judgement many and various are the reasons for which people self-harm all of them to be taken seriously and addressed in their own right.

<u>A reason to love them</u> - In this chapter, the 'them' might be not so easy to spot as the subject is, the self. I could choose to discuss 'them' as those who's teachings have led us to behave or feel in a manner that caused us to self-abuse or harm ourselves, those who have either enabled us or those who have not supported or helped us during those times we turned on ourselves. Instead

I am going to approach this from a different angle. The 'them' in this chapter, are us. The inner part of ourselves that has learnt and chosen to harm us, to judge us, to reject us if we do not play accordingly to the rigid rules and regulations it has come to believe makes us acceptable and lovable. I am going to call this part of ourselves, 'them', The Struggler.

Although one might be forgiven for assuming the *Struggler*, as the name suggests, to be a negative, a 'bad' part of us, a part of us that therefore should be obliterated; I am actually going to introduce it to you under a different light. This *Struggler* part of us, is in fact a great teacher. It plays a great part in our social, physical, emotional and spiritual growth. The *Struggler* is the part of us which although, in appearance, is keeping us growing through struggle and hardship, all it is actually trying to do is keep us safe, well and protected according to the rules, boundaries, and beliefs we have fed to it over the years. The *Struggler* is very loyal. It is a statistician, after taking all the information it has been given into account, it comes up with the safest route for us to be kept in check and within the conforming regulations. It is up to us to filter new information to the *Struggler* so to achieve different outcomes. It is up to us to inform it that we want to play by different rules, that it's okay to stray from the norm, that it's okay to try new things; to give it a new set of rules for the game that is our life.

There is a hypnotherapy exercise I do with my clients where I take them to meet the *Struggler*. The subconscious encounters they share with me after these sessions are absolutely amazing. In this exercise, the client is encouraged (in their own mind using their imagination) to 'meet and talk' with their inner *Struggler*, allowing their subconscious mind to give it a form, telling it that they now want to grow through happiness and joy and asking the *Struggler* to join them in this new way of growing. The client is then guided to subconsciously deal with any reservations the *Struggler* might have, based on accumulated beliefs and fears stemming from those beliefs. Finally, the client is asked to 'see' the *Struggler* change its form, to accept and absorb this part of themselves, to become one with it, working together as one, to achieve their happiest and healthiest level.

This is yet another way to take back our power, to take responsibility. Yes of course we could blame everyone else for our beliefs and the way we feel and act … but in reality, ultimately it is our choice to absorb these outer influences. It may be that our immediate surroundings, and daily routines put the squeeze on us and brainwash us with certain information, beliefs and ways. However, I believe this to be a poor excuse on our part, to relinquish responsibility, when we take into account that we live in an open culture where we have access to so many channels of information i.e. schooling, friendship groups, media and so on, all different inputs full of alternative choices. We are constantly shown different ideas, beliefs and ways and at the end of the day the final choice rests with us; WE choose what to believe, WE choose how we treat ourselves.

Chapter Five

Giving the Power Away

Now, let me tell you, I am an absolute master at this! Or at least I have been for the majority of my life. Throughout my life I have given away my power as if it was going out of fashion. Whether it was people, animals or situations that asked or did not ask for it, I handed it out like smarties.

From a young age beginning with my father, followed by the nuns in the convent school and then my friends, my need to please and keep people happy, my need to be liked and accepted, made it a daily practice and one of the biggest addictions in my life. I raised pretty much everybody and put them on a pedestal where from the bottom I could look up and see their 'happiness', their power spill over and crush me. As time passed and I got better in my practice I extended this 'gift' to boyfriends, husband, colleagues, bosses and even a complete stranger in a supermarket that for whatever reason decided to have a pop at me. I smiled and apologised for even breathing! Over all those years, I had no clue that I was in part enabling the way I was being treated. I had no idea that I had a say, that I had the power to set a different setting, to bring about a different outcome. It is very true that we can't change people, but it is also very true that if we change ourselves, the way we behave, what we accept and don't accept, the people around us change. Every time I gave away my power (and let's face it, if offered who is going to turn it down?!), under the illusion of making others happy by not disagreeing or by allowing them to stomp on me, not only I was relinquishing my responsibilities of setting my boundaries and allowing self-growth as well as promoting the growth and learning of others, I was choosing to allow unacceptable behaviour, comments and ill intention to come my way. In so doing, I was in fact reinforcing my lack of self-worth whilst training others to disrespect me. I always have had an issue with setting boundaries, I have always held the belief that putting them in place would make me look selfish and unlikable, a belief formed no doubt, out of having been raised in environments where love was conditional and to have an opinion is a sin.

We give the power away in so many different ways, in so many different places, times and situations. This will no doubt raise a few eyebrows, but it is my opinion and finally having learnt that I am entitled to have one, I am expressing it as such. I dare to say that I even gave the power away to the man that attacked me and raped me three times at knife point. I have come to believe that I have done so every time I have come to see myself as a victim instead of as a survivor, every time I have thought of him, pointed my finger at him for me being stuck, depressed and making 'bad choices', with my life. Every time I allowed hate and anger to hold me back from living my life instead of forgiveness and self-love to guide me forward, I gave my power away to him and to the 'incident'.

Using my relationship with my ex-husband as an example; I can choose to blame him, I can choose to tell myself that he put me through hell, that he ruined my pregnancy experiences by inflicting terror upon me, that he has humiliated me on so many occasions... I can point that finger and cry about how he victimised me and robbed me of precious years of my life, of the precious years with my children as babies. Or, I can take responsibility for the part I played in that relationship. Although I might have not realised it at the time, I did have choices. Some choices would not have been good to take as I would have further endangered my life and my children's life, but I always had a choice. Letting fear rule over me, I chose to stay for as long as I did, I chose to justify, excuse, tidy up the destruction he left behind, I chose not to love me enough to say I deserve better. Yes, I was afraid, I was very afraid, but fear is thought based; danger is different. Instead of fearful thought which served to keep me prisoner to keep me stuck, I could have chosen thoughts that empowered me and make me walk away, but I chose the first because at the time, doing my best, settled into what I knew best, pleasing and raising others higher, as my understanding of the role of my life was that I could only ever be a supporting act never the star, not even in my own movie… my life. Hence why I was able to break through that fear for the sake of my sons but not for myself. Whether I like it or not I played my part in that relationship. We play our part in *every* relationship.

Trust me when I say, this is not a judgement toward me or how I have lived my life, as I know that, like all others, I have done (and always do) the best I could with the information I had at the time. I am saying this to drive home the point that when we point a finger and we ignore our own part in any given scenario, we give away our power. When we stop ourselves from living in fear-based emotions and seeing the world from a perspective of hopelessness, when we choose to take responsibility for our own part in the play that is our life, we take our power back. I have come to believe that, no matter what the situation, every time we look to blame, every time we look to see the 'problem' from the outside-in, every time we are faced with a situation that raises a personal inner reaction, and try to solve it from the outside, we give our power away. When we focus on us, when we take responsibility for the part we play in this movie that is our life, we take our power back. That is when we finally believe that it is up to us to create the next step, the next chapter, the rest of our life; then we take our power back.

A reason to love them - As I have translated years of my life into beliefs of unworthiness, being unlovable and insignificant, thus diminishing myself as I entered each relationship throughout most of my life, romantic or otherwise, the perpetrators would have shaped their own. They too would have formed their interpretations and self-sabotaging techniques, views and mannerisms that reflected the path they came to walk. For example, after the attack, I could have chosen to spend the rest of my life as a victim, I could have chosen to see a world where all men were evil, I could have chosen to campaign for all men to be castrated(!) and live a life of anger and bitterness trying to make every man that dared to step into my path pay for what one 'sick' man did to me. Thank God for me and for all concerned I have chosen to 'see' it from a different perspective and formulate different lessons from that experience. However, not everyone is me and dependant on their situations, views, indoctrination, surroundings and support, others might choose to 'lash out', whilst keeping themselves stuck, hurting themselves and those who they come into contact with. A child who has been abused may grow up as an abuser or carrying the banner for child protection. The outcome would depend on the view, self-talk and stories the person came to believe as *their* truth during the time the event took place, and how many of those beliefs were reinforced throughout their life.

The person that chooses to 'take' other people's power, the person who chooses to impose their power through any ill way is a person who has yet to see a way out of their pain... a different point of view... they have not yet found a different story to tell themselves.

At the risk of being controversial again I am going to pose a few questions as food for thought... Without these people how are we going to learn to rise up out of our feeling of worthlessness, of insignificance... how do we come to learn to stand up for ourselves, to know about the power that we hold within; how do we come to learn acceptance, compassion and unconditional love... how do we come to discover ourselves?

Everybody plays a part – everybody serves his or her purpose.

Chapter Six

Narcissists and Bullies

Although it is not always clear on where exactly to draw the line, there is a huge difference between self-love, self-respect, self-esteem, self-belief and narcissism. Whilst the first four stem from humility and promote kindness, care, and nurture, narcissism favours dominance and arrogance and encourages negative emotions like envy, rivalry and hostility. The first four in the list are a requirement for a happy, healthy and balanced life, narcissism is a 'stopper'; it hinders emotional growth, personal and interpersonal. Narcissism is a one handed, one sided over inflated self-love which demands a sort of reverence; it uses and (if the effort is not deemed good enough) abuses others. The narcissist is so self-absorbed that they will do pretty much anything to get what they think is their God given right. They are temperamental and easily angered if not supported or are criticised; they will manipulate, bully and punish in order to raise themselves and achieve the recognition, adulation and attention they believe they are owed. The self-crowned 'kings' and 'queens' of this planet.

As per any personality disorder or - if undiagnosed - personality trait; there are different degrees of expression. It can vary from mild to extreme, from those being at the bottom end of the 'narcissist scale' to those at the very top end. I believe I have been fortunate and unfortunate to have encountered, dotted along my lifeline till now, a fair variety; Going in order of their appearance in my life, I shall start with my father.

My father held narcissistic parental values; his love was not unconditional. Although I have no doubt that he did love me, his need to validate his importance, his place as top of the house hold as well as in the social circle, and his need to reaffirm his self-righteous views came at a cost for the likes of us mere mortals that were in his realm. Being raised under his devaluing responses I grew up feeling unloved, insecure and worthless. No matter how hard I tried to get his recognition or how good I did at something, if someone did better than me at that very same task, all my effort would be invalidated. It would be pointed out that I was not the best and my personal success would be discarded, deemed not good enough. One example that comes to mind is of my early years in primary school, year one and two before I was sent to the convent school. I was pretty good, a clever little girl (as I have come to realise now), constant great reports and top two in the class but to my father I was not number one thus, as he pointed out, 'nothing to sing about'. His expectations were high, his moods would swing tremendously especially if he felt undermined in any way or if he felt any of us would put HIS reputation on the line by straying in any way from his own rigid expectations and views. Although from the age of 8 I was sent away to a convent school, my time at home prior to that and on my returns, were spent pacifying explosive situations. These explosions were merely due to family members not upholding my father's beliefs and expectations which needed to be met down to every last detail. This strict regime, conditional love and the forbidding of self-expression led the way for me to self-reject, to foster self-hate for not being good enough at gaining his love and acceptance, a contributing factor no doubt to me falling into depression from a very young age. Without realizing it, as it is a trait with children of parents with narcissistic values, I spent years of my life trying to prove my worth to my father, making every decision with his beliefs, mindset and ways in mind. Spending my life criticising myself and telling myself that I was not good enough at any given opportunity, doing to myself exactly what he did, comparing myself to others and belittling myself. Subconsciously, in order to please him, in a hope for acceptance and unconditional love, I let 'his voice' guide me, my inner self-talk doing an outstanding job at playing these messages back to me like a broken record. For a long time that voice kept me a prisoner trapped in a past that was not just suffocating and hurting me; but was seriously self-destructive. The irony is that I found out after my father passed away that his words, those very words I had been using in my head and I had let steer me throughout the years, did not match what he held in his heart. When my father became bed ridden and suffered from Alzheimer. On one of my visits to the family home in Italy following my divorce; one of my father's good friends that came to say hello divulged to me that my father told him how proud he was that his daughter had moved to England and made a life for herself, learnt a new language (his dream), and was independent. His only regret and fear apparently was the 'nutjob' of a man I married. This I have to say came as a total shock to me as my father never expressed any words of pride toward me to my face and it took that to his grave.

The next narcissist in my life that has drawn the short straw and therefore up for discussion, is Roberto. As those of you who have read my first book know, Roberto (not his real name) was my first real boyfriend. Roberto fits under the 'golden child' umbrella. The child who couldn't do wrong in his parents' eyes; the child who under his parents' idolisation was raised as being flawless and excessively special thus resulting in such an inflated ego. He would find it perpetually hard to maintain it in 'the real world' where everyone's perceptions, priorities and values vary. A person who had been raised with an enormous sense of devotion and reverence will look to replicate that in the wider world and when they realise that they are not getting the same responses out there as they were getting at home, they are made to look at themselves and question their beliefs in their persona, their worth and their place in this magnitude of life. As flaws start to show up in themselves, given that no one is that perfect, they will fight anyone that is shining the torch on the 'imperfections' by daring to either disagree or not being fully devoted to their lives... me. His narcissistic behaviour flared up every time I was not compliant or in agreement with his view; his emotional manipulation and bullying tactics were aggressively dished out to redirect my behaviour to meet his needs and feed his idealised self-perception. I would not be surprised if a large part of my attraction to Roberto was due to his narcissist traits, probably recognising some of my father's narcissistic' trends.

The third example and arguably the most severe narcissist of all the characters in my life, is my ex-husband, Jerry. Jerry (again, not his real name) had very little or no empathy. With a very arrogant approach, Jerry often behaved and talked as if life and everyone in it, owed him. He demanded constant reassurance, proof of love and admiration. He was very jealous and resentful of other people's achievements, properties and accomplishments. He would become very angry and aggressive if things were not about him or his needs; he resented his children taking priority or needing money to be dressed or fed. In order to keep his power, his importance and self-imposed superior status in the family, he would threaten, terrorise and bully us (me in particular as I always shielded the children as much as I could and, at those times I couldn't, I would spend ages trying to reverse any mental manipulation that had come their way). I lived in fears of this man for years trying to pacify and soften his explosions as I did with my father when I was a child; guessing his moods and his needs to avoid confrontation or being at the receiving end of his wrath. His exaggerated achievement and point-blank made-up stories, aimed to shock as well as gain in 'care' and importance, were a very unnerving insight into his erratic and unravelling mind.

A reason to love them - We may be forgiven for thinking that narcissists are very much in love with themselves and in reality, generally, they tend to hold a very poor self-image of themselves and have low self-esteem. Their constant need for approval and validation from the outside world (which never fulfils them as they struggle to believe it), their need to exaggerate their abilities and achievements, their 'loud' approach whether in 'bigging' themselves up or tearing someone down, serves to support this point.

Researchers seem to agree that narcissistic traits take form after birth and not before (which again reinforces my point that no one is born bad). The understanding is that the behaviour of the adult with narcissistic traits is the outcome of how they have come to view the world based on their past experiences, for example, parenting styles such as spoiling, neglect, insisting on toughness, winning, perfectionism and encouraging entitlement or something that rips through their world as they know it like a life changing traumatic event.

Yes, granted, there are people that can be raised within the parenting home I have just illustrated and that have gone through one or several traumatic events (I for one) and chose a softer, more loving approach to living life. If I were to look into my interactions with my ex-husband and how 'A Reason to Love Them' would apply, I can present you with this, hopefully thought-provoking, view. Indirectly, I have come to know some of the experiences that Jerry endured as a child which would definitely explain how his traits have come to take form but that is a story for him to tell not me. On the other hand, you 'know' me and my past experiences by now (if not, you may want to read my first book 'A Reason to Love Me' and you will get my in-depth life story!). Through how we have experienced our pasts in our own unique ways and viewpoints, Jerry and I have become the people that we are today, but more importantly for the purpose of this exercise, the people that came to meet and marry those years back. Two opposite sides of a spectrum; one a pleaser and a doormat - me, the other a power freak with all his narcissistic traits - Jerry. If we look closely both are very unhealthy approaches to life and the challenges every day presents. His, unhealthy for obvious reasons as his behaviour was a clear display of causing harm, arrogance, control and inflicting terror. Mine maybe not so clear, as at first glance one can see my role as a 'victim', but I dare to say, although no doubt yet again controversial, a 'victim' with a choice. Although from my past I chose the very opposite lesson than Jerry did, while not directly harmful to others I was still hurting others by taking on the role of the *enabler*. By excusing his hurtful behaviour and allowing him to treat me the way that he did, by staying, I was reinforcing his understanding that his actions were okay. We all do the best we can with the information and lessons we have at the time, and on my part, at the time I was driven by fear and the need to 'fix' others. Here were two people, two colossal opposites of learning from their past... but is it possible that maybe that is why our paths crossed? Is it possible that in order for each one of us unique souls to grow in our human experience, we needed to have different people learning in different ways, so we can teach each other and learn from one another? Did we actually need to experience one another to direct us to find the balance, that blissful middle ground? Again, do we need the likes of Jerry to bring a Daniela to realise her own strength when she refuses to see it time and time again through lighter lessons? Do we need a Daniela to show Jerry how harmful his behaviour can be and the heavy cost of the refusal to change... love, family, closeness in exchange for a lonely, sad, angry life?

Was his choice of creating an alternative reality and assuming narcissistic traits and my choice to rescue, a conscious choice or as a result of a blueprint response, an inner instinctive response to guide us to meet each other and walk the path we have come to walk, to play a part we have come to play to impart and receive lessons valuable to our growth?

Food for thought...

Chapter Seven

Emotional Black Mail

Emotional blackmail is a tool that is used on most of us and in turn, most of us, mainly unconsciously learn to use from a very young age. I don't know about you, but I know this strategy has been used on me by most adults in my childhood and in my adult life; and I in turn, looking in retrospect, I found myself using those same sentences I was subjected to, on other people throughout my life, included my children. Until I became aware of it. Ultimately people who use emotional blackmail do so in order to get something they want, sometimes consciously – by mean of manipulation and sometimes unconsciously – by falling into the habit of 'repeat' (repeat sentences or actions that they have observed at some point in their lives). Emotional blackmailers, and here I speak about those that consciously choose to use this approach, usually have low self-esteem and struggle to express their emotions and feelings, thus use this tool, as well as other forms of manipulation (i. e. fear, sadness, hostility…), in order to gain control over situations and/or people.

Emotional blackmail can be expressed in different forms; it can be used as a means to create sorrow for the user, by intimidation, blame or provoking guilt; different ways to coerce the other person to do what they want. "If you don't do that, it means you don't love me", "If you don't come with me, I won't go either... shame, I was really looking forward to it", "I am your mother and still you choose to go and play with your friends instead of being here with me (sad face)", "She's a daddy's girl she prefers to walk by his side rather than mine", "I see how it is, you'd rather do that, than give your friend, your really, really good friend a lift", "That's it, you think about yourself! You wait, this will come back on you and then you'll know how I feel", etc. Just a few mild, yet 'mind-fuck', discombobulating sentences which leave us feeling disconcerted and confused, and often manipulated into pleasing and accommodating the other person; especially if guilt is your forte. Wanting to meet our need to please, our need to be accepted, we find ourselves questioning our 'goodness', questioning whether we, and what we do, is good enough. We question our priorities, we begin to learn that choosing ourselves and our likes is selfish, we start to feed the misconception that prioritising ourselves is wrong; we fall into the ever-decreasing circle of guilt. Bit by bit through trying to avoid these feelings of wrong-doing and guilt, we form the beliefs that others' needs are worth more than ours, sending to the mind the underlining message that we are not worthy or at the very least not as worthy as everyone else... and the pedestal is born. The pedestal, the place where we place everyone on but us; we just stand at the bottom holding it up. Carrying its weight we make it our responsibility to keep it strong and happy, allowing the forever growing gap under the name of being a good human being, at the cost of our needs, self-love and self-care; criteria we have come to believe a worthy price to pay for maintaining others' happiness. All of this happening takes place in our minds without us even realising, especially since, as children we don't question, we tend to follow by example, and our communications skills are generally limited. Emotional blackmailers try and influence our choices and depending on our level of self-worth, the network we have and the beliefs we have formed it can be easier or harder for the manipulation to penetrate our defences and work on us.

Having done a lot of soul-searching and work on myself, which has brought me to gain a healthier mindset, I have come to appreciate that there is a big difference between being of service to people and raising people through healthy support, and being a servant and raising people by keeping ourselves down by enabling unhealthy behaviour. First of all, we are not responsible for others' happiness, their happiness is owned and maintained by their mindset, and how they choose to see life. Secondly, respect for our individuality, our ways, opinions, views, lessons learnt in time, and journeys are our right, not someone else's assumption of how we should or shouldn't be. It is not up for anyone else's scrutiny, taking or changing or imposing a different version of ourselves. Furthermore, emotional blackmail is a bully's game and it is our responsibility, as soon as we realize we are the recipients of such a game, to not indulge or enable the perpetrators, but to stand up for ourselves, because every time we do right by us, every time we make ourselves respected, we teach others how we like them to interact with us; perhaps in a way that they are not yet accustomed to.

<u>A reason to love them</u> - Whether consciously or unconsciously, the perpetrators in charge of emotional blackmail have learnt this trait, they did not own it at birth. If each one of us looks deeper into our life, I can guarantee that at some point we too have used this method to get what we wanted, whether as a child, as an adult or both. Whilst some people make this trait a way of life, many of us when we notice the affect that such a behaviour has on others, especially our loved ones, work on finding a different way to achieve our targets. For those who don't, is it possible that for now they have not yet had their eyes opened to the harmful results of this choice of behaviour? Is it possible that their understanding and growth time has not yet arrived? Is it possible that too many of us because of our beliefs keep bowing down and enabling these ways? Is it possible that, yet again, some of us are late bloomers in gathering life lessons so that we can, through our wrong doings help open as many eyes as possible to the recognition of self-worth, self-love and self-respect? Perhaps, as the saying goes, everyone else is a mirror of ourselves, instead of focussing on these people's behaviour to pass on judgement, we could use it for learning to better ourselves and how we communicate. We could use it for self-discovery, after all, we are responsible for our actions, reactions, emotions and feelings. If we can be easily manipulated it might be wise to look within ourselves at how, where and why we have taken on board the opinion that our ways and our beings need to be validated, accepted and approved by someone on a different journey who knows nothing about us. It is not the perpetrator that takes our power away and can make us feel like a victim, it is ourselves who hand them that power.

Chapter Eight

Friendships

There has been a plethora of research projects and books written about and commentaries that have dissected, delved into and debated this Pandora's Box and plenty more that can still be said on this subject as the many trains of thought continue to vie for superiority! I think over the years I have come across many different shades of friendship some of them fitting the bill of the characters mentioned in other chapters in this book; others, angels walking on earth. My very first friendship was a healthy loving one. A true, balanced (apart from some of the times when the adults got involved), close, warm friendship, with our family neighbours' daughter from a very young age, Romina. A friendship which very few people came close to matching in purity ever since. With this experience of friendship as a role model, freely expressed, mostly with no adults playing games to feed their ego, roaming the vast countryside, no need to outdo or impress one another, it can be a bit of a shock when you are thrown into a totally opposite scenario and you are presented with a new definition of friendship. 'Thrown' into a place to live with other children from a variety of backgrounds, in a close environment, with manipulating adults constantly picking at things and breathing down your neck; a place where children, although underhandedly, were encouraged to fight one another for love, recognition, validation, acceptance and importance - the convent school I was sent to. Of course, there were other shades of friendship in between these two examples but I believe these were the two strongest influences in forming my opinion on friendships. I believe these were the bases that steered me to understand what I needed in a friend, my preferences; they shaped my level of trust or lack of, which I would come to dish out to others in years to come.

Having lived in varied institutions, and 'intense' cultural and religious settings I have come to form, like a lot of people, friendships that last a life time, regardless of how many times you speak or see each other and others that dissolve in the winds of time and the connection is never rekindled.

Time and controversy test the strength of a relationship, some withstand the strongest storms standing shoulder to shoulder with you while others fall away at the first hurdle. One statement that is often used is "you know who your friends are in your time of need" but rarely we come to mention what I have also come to experience, "you know who your friends are in your time of joy". We form friendships with people that stand by us no matter what we do 'good' or 'bad'; friendships which we truly give ourselves to.

Friendships which we fully trust, and we would give our life for. Then we have the other type of friendships those that are of convenience and friendships which we use to measure our power, our worth upon. Friendships who we willingly throw away over a man, a woman, money, status, the next shiny situation that turns our head. I personally struggle to throw away anything and despite of what comes to play, rightly or wrongly, although I have got a little better over the years at setting up boundaries to limit emotional damage, I never fully shut any door, so when this last one takes place I feel the sting and it takes me a while to reason within my head, to remind myself that the other person's behaviour is not a reflection of me but of their own beliefs, self-worth, values and the path they are on.

As this book is aimed at finding a reason to love the perpetrators, these 'plastic' friendships are the ones we shall have a closer look at.

It is perfectly normal to have different level of closeness with different people as we tend to strike more of a rapport and understanding with those we have more in common with; the better the matching of our likes, dislikes, beliefs, dreams and ideologies the closer the bond. It is also perfectly normal to have friends that we go to the movies with, others clubbing, and others you play mah-jong with as our individuality causes us to like certain things and not others and what some of our friends might enjoy others might not. If everyone accepted and respected this level of exchange, uniqueness and carried the flag for 'I am there for you – you are there for me', 'Love without condition' and 'Live and let live' we would all have a smoother ride, but us being human we don't do many things the easy way... we complicate. Jealousy, ego, inferiority/superiority complexes, low self-esteem... everything is a competition to better one another. Then you have those people that are so self-absorbed and afraid of drowning in their own mess that only come to us for help, only ever when they need something, at all other times you are invisible to them, they are too busy playing catch up with themselves. In my life I have had 'friends' who would have had lions eat me in order to save their skin, others who simply threw me to the lions even if their skin was not in need of saving. I have had friends that left me to drown in my pit of sorrow and others that cut me out at the moment they saw me rise up. How much of their behaviour has anything to do with me? All of it and none of it. My understanding and opinion is that their behaviour, their intention, their doing, the part they play, is theirs, nothing to do with me; on the other hand, what I allow, how I receive it, how I allow it to affect or not to affect me, is my responsibility.

A reason to love them - I have already mentioned some of the' kiss of death' scenarios that occur and cause the dissolving or erosion of friendships (and any type of relationship): -jealousy, ego, inferiority complex, superiority complexes, low self-esteem and to add a few more- comparison, lack of confidence and fear. As common practice goes, most of us have learnt to look at problems and situations from the outside in. When we hurt, we quickly turn to see where we can point the finger or where the other person did wrong. Although at times there is nothing in our 'physical action' that warrants the other person to act hurtfully towards us, a lot of the time we have played a role. Still forgetting that we can only tend to ourselves in the lesson that shows us when a change of behaviour and growth is due, blinkered we charge ahead to look for the faults in the other person, rather than in the part we played.

Although I consider myself a good friend to all who would have me, there is no shadow of a doubt in my mind that because of misunderstandings, differences in opinion and/or allowing one or more of the conditions from the 'kiss of death list', to dwell in my mind, someone somewhere in my past will say that I came up short in some respects at being their friend; equally there may have been times when I thought so too of them. This will always happen. With each of us having different beliefs, understanding and often the expectations of what everyone should do, be and think the way we do, we come to see situations from different perspectives. Communication and honesty, gifts that not many of us have come to master and are yet so essential in our capacity to understand, recover and manage a crisis, seem to elude or frighten us.

He who hath never sinned cast the first stone! How many of us can say that we have always been fully truthful to our friends, that we have never done them wrong, no matter how little or unintentional the action or word. The argument is, I hear some people say, that there are people that are very aware of their actions, words and intentions and still behave in such a manner. Point taken; but can we maybe take notice that on our road of learning we all screw up at some point or another and, although most of us learn the lesson, some of us might need a few extra takes before we grasp it. Also, why are we so focussed on their learning instead of our own? Why instead of seeing where they are going wrong, are we not focussing on the part we play whilst we are allowing it… why are we allowing it? Why are we not speaking up for ourselves, why are we not expanding our communication skills? And what lesson can WE take from this.

If we look at each event through the lens of 'looking for the lessons' instead of who is the most righteous we would shed a lot of the pain, we get to see humanity in the other person and we get to focus on the life we want to live. This life has been entrusted to us with its own unique blueprint to build on and develop our understanding of humanity and to share our gifts with those that we come into contact with.

Our friends, those who still stand with us, those who have become a little loose and those that have become estranged, are, like us trying to get to know themselves and their intricate interaction with others in the world a little better. Sometimes getting it right, sometimes getting it wrong, sometimes regretting decisions, actions taken, or words spoken… sometimes not. All depending on the crutches, walls, baggage, beliefs, fears and mixture of limitations we have brought into play on our own journeys. Everyone fights battles and makes decisions through a perspective the others in their circles know nothing about.

Chapter Nine

Relationships

Relationship is a sweeping, general term that encapsulates any sort of interaction between beings. As I have addressed friendship, the relationships I am going to address here is the romantic type. The one where two consensual individuals fall in love and at some point, one of the parties 'earns' the label of perpetrator having inflicted pain whether emotional or physical on the other person.

When we enter a relationship, we all carry a bagful of unique understandings, learning, likes, dislikes, gems and ammunition that we have collected along the path we have walked and experienced through the trials and tribulations and situations we have been dealt. Healthy or unhealthy the collection, both parties enter the relationship with a set view. To add to the baggage that we enter our relationships with, is the time and the changes it brings as we live our days together. Relationships come to shoulder the wrath of time, as human beings we change, we evolve, we experience, we discover... new jobs, new friends, new style of clothes, new drinks, new food. . . as we go through these changes, through the different influences, through temptations, or even through key life changing events like menopause we might not grow at the same rate as our significant others.

If we start from the beginning of a relationship, the majority of people when they first come together are on their best behaviour, the 'Honeymoon Period'. In order to impress, to be liked, they put on show the best version of themselves; holding back on the little (or big) habits that they would otherwise display in a more ordinary, more comfortable situation, with a long-standing friend for example. We might show ourselves tidier, make more effort with our appearance, we might try to be more gentlemanly more ladylike or more disciplined with our eating habits. Whatever would allow us to be perceived in a good light to attract and win the object of our desire. However, any behaviour that is not customary to our way and that demands a certain level of tension and alertness does not last forever and tends to revert back to our preferred way. Whilst at the beginning of a relationship we are not living together and we are not constantly in each other's pocket, and have lots of down time to retreat into our relax states, our own comfort zone and way of being, dreaming happily about this new wonderful person we have met, once the relationship is in full swing we haven't got these 'respite' breaks and sooner or later we display them in front of our new partner. At the end of the day we all like to live in comfort and in a relaxing environment, whatever that means to each of us. Let's use a dinner date as an example; lateness in the early stages of a relationship and lateness in a relationship that is established. In the first scenario, we meet someone and we invite them over for a meal. They are almost an hour late, and they haven't called. When they arrive, they apologise, they explain what held them back and come in. Prior to this, whilst still checking that all is in order for the twentieth time, we might have been stressing, worrying that the meal is going to be ruined, wondering what the hell they are playing at, telling ourselves how rude that they haven't had the decency to even give us a call or send us a text. Still we let them in, smile on our faces, glad and grateful that they are here now, we quickly let it go and we get engrossed in our evening. A totally different story ten years later when we have married this person; same scenario, different welcome and outcome. Now the story we tell ourselves is somewhat different; we might have those same stressful, annoyed thoughts, but instead of the grateful and relieved response, we proceed to add a few more negative points: - 'he is taking me for granted', 'she has no appreciation for all I do', 'he doesn't care', 'Does she think I'm stupid' etc. and forgiveness, acceptance, relief and understanding go out of the window, and instead of welcoming them home and getting on with a nice evening we hold a grudge and wear a long face for the next three days so not to let them forget their inconsiderate behaviour. Why is it that what we allowed then is not acceptable now?

Borders get crossed, responsibility lines get blurred, priorities change, expectations grow. Often, as times goes by and the relationship progresses, we develop a sense of entitlement, of possession. Unhealthily we become addicted to the other person and we fear losing them, so the pressure is on. Feeling exposed, our mind runs through thousands of scenarios where we tell ourselves all sorts of horror stories. Stories where we tell ourselves that maybe we are no longer good enough or important enough to our loved one; convincing ourselves that they are not so keen on us anymore, that they are so bored with us that they would rather spend their time elsewhere. Maybe even that they have already substituted us with someone better/younger/fitter and concealed it behind lies and excuses and enraged we tell ourselves that they think of us as fools. The spiral can go on and on; the stories we can tell ourselves when we feel vulnerable are varied in weight and direction. In all cases we end up projecting these fears, these negative views and thoughts onto the latecomer and the evening has come to an end even before it begins. With the barriers we raise by feeding our demons, with the growing of expectations, with the lack of communication which serves to feed misunderstandings, we grow apart. We start noticing that our wife does not laugh as freely like the girl in the office, we start wishing that our husband was as kind and supportive as someone who wrote on a Facebook status, we start investing less in this relationship and look for the escape often without trying, understanding or addressing the issues. Unfortunately, most of us live out our relationships in our head instead of in actual fact or reality; so not surprisingly, as the human mind has been mainly domesticated to think negatively and to come from a place of fear, this causes more problems than resolutions. We really must practice and get better at – thinking less and conversing more. Mind reading, jumping to conclusions and awfulizing are some of the worse thinking errors we tend to drop into. Real menaces in any form of relationship.

As I have already mentioned, we enter each relationship with a preselected view and expectation, and it is on this basis that we play our role.

In my studies as a counsellor I have come across 'The Karpman Drama Triangle' which reflects and illustrates beautifully and clearly how most people in a relationship come to interact by moving within the following roles: - Rescuer, Persecutor and Victim. (There is a really good article online called The Relationship Triangle if you would like to have a deeper understanding of how this works on https://www. psychologytoday. com/blog/ fixing-families/201106/the-relationship-triangle)

Although we move within these roles, there is generally one that fits better, and we spend more time playing, than the others.

Now although this interchange between these roles are very normal and very human, the unhealthier the persons emotional state the more extreme the behaviour and the length he or she stays in the persecutor state; regardless of if he or she comes from the rescuer or the victim position.

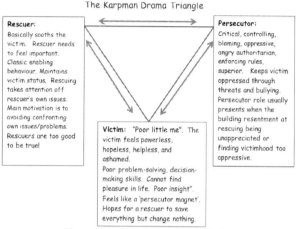

The Karpman Drama Triangle

Rescuer:
Basically sooths the victim. Rescuer needs to feel important. Classic enabling behaviour. Maintains victim status. Rescuing takes attention off rescuer's own issues. Main motivation is to avoiding confronting own issues/problems. Rescuers are too good to be true!

Persecutor:
Critical, controlling, blaming, oppressive, angry authoritarian, enforcing rules, superior. Keeps victim oppressed through threats and bullying. Persecutor role usually presents when the building resentment at rescuing being unappreciated or finding victimhood too oppressive.

Victim: "Poor little me". The victim feels powerless, hopeless, helpless, and ashamed.
Poor problem-solving, decision-making skills. Cannot find pleasure in life. Poor insight". Feels like a 'persecutor magnet'. Hopes for a rescuer to save everything but change nothing.

These roles or feeling states rotate in time!

When I first came across The Karpman Drama Triangle I truly had a 'light bulb' moment; everything kind of made sense, I could see relationships clearly. I could see MY part in each relationship I have been in, as clear as day and the empowerment I got from this revelation, this understanding, this penny dropping moment, has been massive for me. The introspection it brought has been a breath of fresh air, to me a massive weight off my shoulders. After all the years of being swallowed by the fog, my misty mind stuck in search for answers, years under the weight of the huge umbrella of 'Whys' now finally I could see a clear blue sky with no ambiguity. We all need different pieces to complete our jigsaw puzzle of questions, for me on this matter, it was this one.

A reason to love them - Based on personal experiences and avoiding any fluff filled and complicated terms, I am going to describe the perpetrator in relationships as someone who is in pain and/or is very scared; and takes action to control that pain and fear by harming those they love.

We are all very quick to see the negative actions and words of the 'relationship' perpetrator but what we often fail to see is the reasons behind those very actions and words. Please do not mistake this statement as an excuse for their behaviour, having been on the receiving end of some very nasty expressions and explosions of someone experiencing such a turbulent state of mind, I know that it is inexcusable; yet, I believe, understandable and thus forgivable. Before your track me down and throw this book at me, I ask that you open your mind to a different perception for just a moment. What if we saw the wounds in that person? What if we saw the fear that paralyses them and causes them to lash out? What if we saw the travelling, learning soul… what if we saw our son, daughter, or ourselves in that struggling mindset? Would we be so quick to judge? What I am saying here, is not to stay with this person and abdicate your happiness or dedicate your life to help, 'fix', the perpetrator; because this is not your job. Their happiness belongs to them, we are not responsible for other people's happiness and they are not responsible for ours. True happiness can only be harvested from within not from the outside that can make it all weather dependant. In fact, by staying, often we end up enabling that behaviour. No, I am saying this, to help you rid yourself of the attachment to drama, anger and judgement; to remind you once more that these emotions only serve to keep us stuck, they distract us from the focus that is living our own life to the fullest, in this very moment; not spending it cursing someone else who is fighting battles that only they can appreciate the true depth of. We always have a choice to leave; but we don't truly leave them if we spend our time thinking how they have done us wrong. They, on the other hand, can never leave themselves they can only decide to step away from that fear and that pain, grow and change but they cannot leave themselves no matter how long it takes for them to learn those lessons.

Work on what can be worked upon and discover what compromises can be found; leave without judgement and anger after those times when resolutions are unattainable, and you'll find yourself freeing yourself.

A handful of compassion bound with self-focus: - focus on our life, our path, our purpose and on our self-building will free both parties to live the life we have come to play out, without the need to step into judgement or criticism; keeping us away from falling into the trap of directing someone else's life; their path. Their life doesn't belong to us.

Chapter Ten

Domestic Violence

When we hear the term domestic violence, we immediately see in our heads, images of women with bruises; but domestic violence incorporates so much more than that. For a start domestic violence is not just a term that refers to women. Many men wear this cap and fit into this category, under this umbrella. To touch on the coverage of this term, besides the physical, domestic violence encases several aspects, including: - psychological, sexual, emotional and financial. Any act of force, manipulation, controlling behaviour that regularly constricts and regulates one's behaviour; exploitation, coercion, threats, intimidation, humiliation and other ways that are used to abuse, scare, punish and/or harm another person (over 16 years of age) in the home.

I first witnessed domestic violence in my childhood, although at the time besides knowing that what was taking place was and felt wrong, I did not know it under this label. The screaming, the verbal abuse, the intimidating looks, threatening vocabulary and body language I saw, as the people within my home of origin, namely my parents, my granddad and my uncle who lived with us, were tearing each other apart, looking back, was actually outrageous. Then there was the physical type when my dad would give my mother not only a piece of his mind but would follow up with a slap. As a very sensitive little girl, feeling tenfold the pain of this disharmony and this aggressive expression of character and points of view, many were the times where I played the role of the rescuer and desperately tried to diffuse the situations but with little change or results. As it is often said, as we grow older, we tend to recreate relationships with people that reflect those from our childhood; subconsciously trying to fix the unfixable. Following in this pattern in my adult life, I engaged and formed relationships with people that embodied those characteristics and way of expression that were the dynamics in my household then. Consciously unaware, I attracted these challenges with an inner belief of 'fix this now fix the past'. I attracted relationships where I was physically abused – and I could not fix them, then or those from the past; I attracted relationships where I was psychologically abused – and I could not fix them or those from past; I attracted relationships like in the case of my ex-husband, which fitted pretty much all of the descriptions I have given of the recount of my family of origin – and I could not fix that either. The only thing that helped me was to leave each one of these people; focus on me, my growth my worth. Having lived through these experiences and becoming aware of the patterns, it has helped me to consciously understand that what I was subconsciously replaying in my life was not only futile but was seriously unhealthy for me. Understanding and choosing not to live my life on the back of a past that could never be changed, and live by outdated beliefs formed at those times, I eventually learned to know my worth, my value and my power. This in turn served me to attract a different partner with a different character, values, ways and a more balanced mindset thus creating a healthier family setting.

It is obviously much easier to evaluate my involvement in each of the situations I found myself in and recount it with a cooler perspective, especially after years of being detached from those moments, gaining a qualification in counselling and various therapies as well as continually learning, by means of self-improvement materials as well as positive life experiences. At the time however, I did not have any of this knowledge and I had not come to experience anything different that would make me 'see' anything other than the life I had manifested. I did not know I had a choice; and the belief that I could fix 'it', that I could fix them kept me trapped. Now I know I was keeping me trapped. I kept me trapped with the beliefs that I had come to form and the stories that I would tell myself with my thinking. Granted, a lot of those stories were based on some very true events. Readdressing and expanding in my relationship with my ex-husband as an example, he did try to strangle me, in a fit of jealousy he did attempt to drive me and our children off the road, he did regularly threaten my life, he did isolate me from the rest of the world, constantly checking-up on me and returning me home every time I was in someone else's company or house, including his own family or the park if I took the children out for a play away from our home. He did manipulate me and used my experience of being raped, prior to us meeting, against me, in order to keep me frightened of the outside world and under his full power and control. In drunken states he would turn our house upside down, on one occasion cut himself and smeared his blood all over the walls. On another occasion, whilst at my parents' house in Italy he took my father's hunting shot gun and hid it under the settee waiting to see the outcome of my response following his smashing up of my parents living room and bathroom door. I spent most of my marriage being truly petrified. With this brain washing and my already vulnerable mindset, it was hardly surprising. Many nights spent in fear, drenched in sweat as I would play out in my mind's eye all the horrors that could happen when he got upstairs to our bedroom, how drunk would he be? Would he try to strangle me again? Would he kick another hole in the door? Although generally he takes it out of me, are the children safe? Am I going to be alive in the morning? All valid questions considering the environment I was living in but controversial or not, I now know and believe, that it was I that kept me trapped in that life not him. In none of those questions that I was asking myself was anything empowering, I was coming from a fear-based mindset not from a solution one. A vicious circle that served to reinforce my thoughts of weakness and powerlessness. I could have chosen in those moments to empower myself but instead I chose (unknowingly at the time) to give him the power. Things only changed at the moment I changed my thinking, faced my fears, looked at things from a different perspective, took my power back and left that toxic environment and relationship. Those painful, scary, haunting moments of my experience of domestic violence have contributed to me being the strong woman that I am today and I accept it as an experience that I needed to have as part of my understanding of me, my life and my exchanges within a relationship; as well as gathering and experiencing the emotional and physical trauma to aid me in my purpose to help others as a counsellor and guide today. There is a purpose for everything, even for those times that we live in a state of horror; we learn, and we grow. This recount is not intended to point a finger or place blame, I am just telling it to outline my part and my options under a domestic violence scenario. I am just using it as a point of evidence of how things come to take place, how life always comes to play out, without realizing, we find ourselves in certain roles and situations. Through no fault of our own, we find ourselves there, yet, at the same time we are there as a result of our own choices and life manifestation. We are only ever one thought, one decision, one action away from a place of feeling and being, okay.

<u>A reason to love them</u> - The perpetrator in domestic violence is a person in fear and in pain (although when they express such anger and aggression one would be forgiven for struggling to see these traits); they have low self-esteem, low self-worth and although they seem to advocate the opposite, they have a very low opinion of themselves, their capabilities and their position in the world. Their battle is a constant battle of having to show their value to the world often by telling whopping lies (I know my ex-husband exceeded at this), but these lies are only a confirmation of their tormented mindset and their need to hide it; a mask used to cover up what they are afraid to face up to themselves. Their explosions are an indication of the volcano within, of their inability to soothe that pain, those fears. Life would have knocked at these people's door with various opportunities, situations and chances, for them to face themselves, to grow, to address their ways, feelings and thoughts, beliefs and actions. Opportunities to make choices to shape their ways into a happier and healthier path, to make a choice, to leave the fear behind, to discover who they are. However, their resistance to let go and come away from the habitual feeling of unworthiness, inner as well as outer fights, and denial, is stronger than their willingness and trust to take those opportunities, so they struggle to let go; BOOM is the result. These explosions are the outcome of resisting growth, change, and to allow oneself to mature, to develop self-acceptance, trust and self-love. Choosing to dig their heals in, not taking responsibility for their lives, and when the inner fight gets too much, unwilling and fearful to open the mythical Pandora's Box and look within, they place the blame on the outside world and take their anger out on their loved ones.

This is their battle and nothing any of us caught in these types of relationships can do to make them change unless they choose to. Their outbursts have nothing to do with us, they are not an indication of what we did wrong or what we did not do; it is not a reflection on us but of them and their head space. Whilst we may try at first to smooth over these episodes, accommodate, talk through things, and even offer some helpful techniques and reassurance, if the person does not change their way, we need to stop this approach. If we keep reassuring, excusing and picking up the pieces, instead of helping them stop, we end up sending the signal that it's okay and indirectly validate their actions; we become the enabler. The term being cruel to be kind comes to mind here; and leaving this destructive setting is an act of love toward them as well as ourselves. They deserve better than our help in reinforcing their fears and bad habits and we deserve better than living a life of fear, hurt and emotional abuse at the end of someone who is refusing to learn their lessons to find peace.

Whilst it is important for us to accept another soul's path and the different parts and lessons they have come to live and express as their life; it is also important to accept and understand our part and lesson in this exchange. The acceptance of where they are at, does not mean that we have to endure and stay, our lessons may in fact be one of learning on when to step away from these kinds of relationships. Perhaps our own lessons rest in knowing when to stop 'fixing and rescuing', on when to stop playing the martyr, on when to show ourselves respect, or on when to stand up for ourselves, or even perhaps on better distinguishing between compromising and being a doormat. The lessons are there for us all at any given time, in any interaction. Nothing is for nothing.

The important question here, is whether we stay and try one more time or leave; judgement on the perpetrator will not help us see our way. I now believe that forgiveness and understanding is the only clear pathway in both scenarios. If we stay and try to salvage the relationship one more time, the forgiveness and understanding mindset, will help us see each situation as a unique state, for what it is in the moment it occurs instead of adding to the pain and anger of the previous incidents thus more clearly accessing and dealing with what we are presented instead of the cloudy (at times irrational) response that can come with the addition of blameful recollection. If we leave, forgiveness frees us from the prison of living in what was; in the constant memory of it which often comes with recalling and feeding the anger of how we have been done wrong. It allows us to grow by letting go and taking responsibility for our part and our lessons. With this growth comes the understanding and the reminder that these perpetrators are simply struggling to find their way; wounded animals who have caged themselves and are still in search of a way out. Unrested souls who still can't see the wood for the trees, hiding from their own happiness.

Chapter Eleven

Living in Fear

I think most of us are masters at this. Living in fear is thought generated and as we are all very good at overthinking, we all, at some point or another, find ourselves in the clasp of fear. Whether we experience anxiety, nervousness, a phobic reaction, body or emotional paralysis or any other 'irrational' emotional or physical response, we have tripped on a thought that has caused us alarm. A lot of us are afraid of looking silly, of making mistakes, of making the wrong choices, of losing opportunity, of not being good enough, of breaking a vase that means a lot to grandma and the list goes on. Have you ever thought however, what makes a person afraid of bungy jumping whilst another thrives on it? Or why one person freezes at the sight of a spider and another holds it as a pet? It is the type of thought that we attach to these situations that makes us feel one way or another. If I think of bungy jumping as a feeling of freedom, of an adrenalin rush I can easily get excited about the idea; but on the other hand if I think of the wire or harness snapping or the length required being misjudged and me hitting the ground and dying, well… all of a sudden the excitement disappears and

I am not so keen on giving it a go. The views and the response we have come to adopt are a result of the life experiences, beliefs and influences we have had. When we conclude whether something is good or not so good, dangerous or otherwise, we have zip wired into a past of information and deduced our answer. The problem we might encounter is that although certain situations are proven to be facts i. e. you walk into a tiger's enclosure when this beauty of an animal is just awaiting its breakfast, there is a very high chance you are going to get eaten, others are simply personal truths. A lot of our predicted outcomes are established on the basis of someone else's (parents, teachers, extended family, friends, colleagues, society in general etc.) ideas, experiences, interpretations, words, behaviour or beliefs that would have no relevance to us or our current circumstances; yet we adopt them as a fact. We let them shape our judgement and feed our fears, thus letting them hold us back from making up our own mind and living each situation as our experience. Fear is a product of our thinking, of our imagination left to run wild. To apply this understanding to my life, following on from the previous chapter on domestic violence, I can see, now that there is a distance in time and healing has taken place, how this notion played out then. Recalling the earlier years of my marriage to Jerry where his mental manipulation and threats were strong but had not yet escalated to physical, to a particular time when, pregnant, I was waiting for him to come home from the pub. I was already living in terror before he even got home. The sweats, the tension, the anxious breathing were all side effects of my thinking, of my imagination running from one image of terror to the next. I was living in my mind's eye all kinds of horrible scenarios where I would become an injured (or worse) victim. At that time his physical violence and aggression were aimed at the environment, walls, doors and so on but I had already escalated it in my head to include me. Even in those few times when he came in and fell asleep on the settee watching tv or fully dressed on top of the bed, my mind would run all sort of scenes, including him trying to strangle me in my sleep (and this incident had not yet taken place). As I have previously mentioned, there is a huge difference between fear and danger, whilst danger is factual (you are faced with a tiger... run!), fear lives in the imagination of our thinking. Far too often we use our amazing gift of imagination to infiltrate our own mind with negative images and poison it with terror.

When we live in fear, we act different, we think different, we see different; the energy we send out is different. Have you ever had people tell you, when faced with an aggressive stray dog perhaps, to show no fear, and they are less likely to attack? My sister in law at the time said it best when she told me never to back down in front of her brother, but to stand up to him. Apparently when he did try to enforce his powerful attitude upon her, she responded with chucking plates at him. The message, loud and clear, was go and pick on someone else, this girl does not bow down to your shit. It worked. I on the other hand had not learnt the knack of that yet, and I allowed him to feast on my fear.

Fear is a blood sucking leach. It not only holds us back from reaching our potential, from experimenting, learning and living our life to the full; unbounded, fear makes us an easy target; it makes it easy for manipulators, narcissists, abusers to work on their prey when they are caught up in fear.

How would our lives be transformed if we came from a place of positive possibilities instead of a place of negative 'what ifs'? What if we focussed on solutions instead of feeding our imaginations with ideas that keep us trapped? How many more things would we try? What if instead of being afraid of what people thought for example, we actually saw them trying and failing as we do, in an attempt to align before them a life of enjoyment, wellbeing and richness? Think of the rewards, if we decided to focus on ourselves, on our doings, on our experimenting, on our living, without the distraction of worries, of the fear of getting things wrong and being judged… the advancement and joy this would bring! The undiluted energies directed towards our development, goals and dreams would massively enrich ourselves, our lives and consequently, by default enrich the lives of those around us; enriching our world.

Coming from the premise that we can't give from an empty vessel, what we put in our vessel is what we are able to give. Therefore, it makes sense to deduce that if we fill our vessel with fear that is exactly what we are going to dish out into our lives; if we fill it with love or hope or joy or courage or positivity these are what we will endow our lives with instead. Each day, each moment, we get to choose that which we wish to manifest. What are you filling your vessel with today?

<u>A reason to love them</u> - In this chapter, I identify the perpetrators as pretty much every single one of us.

Every time we step into fear we come away from love and we persecute another living soul, and more often so, ourselves; we are the perpetrators. Fear is behind the actions of every perpetrator. The opposite of love is not hate, it is fear; hate is founded on and fuelled by a fear. When waiting for my ex-husband to come home, running riot with those scary thoughts and images in my head, afraid, I was persecuting myself way before he started. Every time we have a go at someone, about their religion, colour, action, beliefs, opinions, words or anything of any sort, we come from a place of fear. We are fearful of their differences, of their thoughts, of the possible unfamiliar outcomes, of standing out, of being unnoticed, of being ridiculed, of not being accepted... fearful of many things.

In this chapter the caption 'A Reason to Love Them' couldn't be more appropriate or more defining. Hate, anger or other negative emotions cannot drive away the fear, our own or others'; only love can do that. By loving, understanding, seeing the soul, the different paths, the different walks of life we each walk; by being open to other ways, by being curious, ready and willing to discover, with compassion, we eradicate fear. By learning, by seeing the different purposes and journeys that each one of us has come to experience, by allowing ourselves to see from a different angle of the glass and noticing a different image; by seeing this life, not as a threat but as a puzzle, a game of discovery, an amazing maze which will deliver us to new opportunities and understanding ourselves. When we look through the eyes of wonder, we change our perception and therefore our feelings. There are many reasons for which to love ourselves for who we are and the life we have come to live. When we finally decide to pay attention and switch our focus to these reasons and we roll and flow with this amazing feelings, bathing in the understanding and peace they bring, we dismantle fear and we build a stronger sense of love and acceptance that expands to include all others who like us have come to walk this earth.

Chapter Twelve

Responsibilities and Boundaries

M any of us come to experience both, a healthy and 'unhealthy' mindset with regards to responsibilities. We find ourselves battling against a variety of feelings and emotions while attempting to find a balance and an understanding of what is under our care and what isn't. Some of us take on all responsibilities and are crushed under their weight; while some of us wave them all away, then unable to take care of anything, place the blame onto others.

Various are the ways we come to see responsibilities. For a start, there are those responsibilities which, from a young age, we are instructed and informed that they belong to us. Then, there are also those responsibilities that we, ourselves, come to conclude and accept via way of deduction, are ours to bear. Through our 'reading' of people and situations, our need to be helpful, our eagerness to please, aided by any other self-loathing emotional trait we have come to own, we add to the pile of responsibilities that may or may not belong to us.

From when we are young, we are taught to take responsibility through the understanding of those around us. Often however, that teaching is not as clear as it could be, and the meaning and application of this noun gets lost in translation. Somehow in between the spoken words of our educators and their actions and reactions to their life events and circumstances, the message gets clouded. For example, let's say we are at school and don't do well in a test, we go home, and we tell our parents. To our defence, we tell them that the reason for the poor result was that we had not been taught half of the stuff that came up on the test as the subject teacher was out for the whole term and we had a variety of substitute teachers. Their response is that this reason is not a good enough reason as it is our responsibility to communicate, ask the teacher, any teacher, research and learn around the subject to get positive outcome. The day after when that very parent returns home from work and we are sitting at the dinner table having a nice meal, we hear them, whilst seething, talk of an incident at work where they got called into the boss's office for a telling off because they submitted a report that didn't include particular information, things that, in our parents opinion was someone else's job to provide to them. So, we are left totally confused on the double standard message of the reliability and the function of responsibility; as it seems to be okay for our parent to place the blame onto someone else, but it was not acceptable or excusable for us.

This difficulty in understanding where responsibilities lie, is especially true with regard to personal responsibility, emotional as well as practical. These messages tend to become even more incoherent when applied to personal and emotional relationships and situations, when ego comes to join and play its part. On my part I was raised with the understanding that absolutely everything was my responsibility, especially in the days spent in the convent boarding school. Being the daughter of a communist I was always the one assigned with blame, whether the actions or words spoken were my own or otherwise. I learnt to self-loath and to make every situation, every problem, every resolution, every pain, mine. I carried on in this pattern, adding more and more as I went along. As I took on the burdens and responsibility of those around me with the view to help and bring happiness to as many as I could, I began to leave me behind; there simply was not enough time in the day. At times I would spare me a thought when I went to bed at night, but falling under the exhaustion of a heavy mind, I'd soon crash, and I would be once again forgotten. All of this because of an over inflated sense of obligation, an unhealthy understanding of responsibility, an unrestored balance.

On the other hand, there are those who very much welcome the lack of responsibilities. They believe that everything is someone else's fault; that their unhappiness, misfortunes or whatever is not up to scratch in their life is all due to some other person. The culture of pointing fingers is widely practiced and generally overshadows that of taking responsibility.

Maybe it would help if we made the line that separates the two a little clearer.

Our own intention, our thoughts, our words, our actions and reactions, our feelings and our understanding of any given situation belong to us. They are OUR responsibility.

The intention, thoughts, words, actions and reactions, feelings and the understanding of any given situation that any person around us experience and chooses to express belong to them. That is THEIR responsibility.

This is where boundaries are a welcome introduction.

Once we are clear on who is responsible for what, it is important that we learn to put boundaries into place to maintain each other's roles. A way if you will, to ensure a smoother ride for the relationship and our individual selves to grow and develop. First of all, we have to make sure that our boundaries are 'healthy boundaries', that we are not using them as a means to hide ourselves from situations, lessons, or to shut people out. Boundaries are not just something we put in place to keep others from stepping onto our chosen space and growth; they are also something that we need to learn to put in place, so we don't step into others space and growth. If like me you have spent a lot of your life dedicating yourself to rescuing under the illusion of making people happy (I say illusion, because other's happiness belongs to them and therefore, out of our control), this task is not an easy one to start with. As a rescuer, putting a barrier into place to stop yourself from being a doormat or being abused by those who refuse to take responsibility might be a bit of a problem, as this rescuing behaviour and the habit of taking responsibility for everything and everyone is strong and if not kept harnessed will unleash an avalanche of fears. I found that what helped and still helps, on those moments of guilt and finding it hard to let go thus allowing others to take responsibility, is a technique where I look at things from the opposite perspective than the one, I am accustomed to. Instead of looking at how my lack of input makes me unkind and would be bad for them, I look at the situation from the aspect of how my standing back is a bigger act of love. I am loving them enough to let go and allow the other person to self-discover and find their power. I look for aspects that show me why it is for their own good. I take the approach that when I trust in their ability to 'man up' and deal with it, I allow them to grow; when I don't let go and I 'interfere', I hinder their growth. For those of you that are in the midst of fighting the addiction of rescuing and the guilt that comes with stepping away from it, it might take a while to implement this technique, so be patient with yourselves. Although I have implemented this practice for quite some time now, there are still many times where I have to consciously remind myself of the importance of boundaries and stepping back.

A reason to love them - Here the perpetrators can be both parties in a relationship. As I have just described even the person with the best intention can become a perpetrator when we choose to step into action and 'rob' the other person from their right of growth and experience. However, the perpetrator that I choose to bring and hold accountable here is the one that intentionally does not take responsibility for their actions and/or does not respect another person's boundaries in mind body and spirit. The people who have learnt to bulldoze their way through, disrespect, disregard, and trash other peoples will, boundaries, wishes, beliefs, ideas and anything they have come to accept as their view of life and living. Put this way it can be really hard to find a way, a reason to love such individuals, but, what other than love can change this pattern? An eye for an eye is not going to work as hate met with hate, has proved itself time and time again to be ineffective to bring peaceful and loving resolution, with a sea of debris in its path; thus, matching a negative emotion and action will not give a positive emotion or outcome. Besides, are these people really aware of their behaviour and impact? What if this is their only known way to interact with another? What if, as an opposite to the example I have given above with regards to the rescuer, they too have an emotion to which they are attached and are stuck with? Maybe not guilt but maybe fear of failing, not getting the result they want or need, being left alone, falling in the depths of that feeling of not being good enough… whatever. Again, there are so many fingers we can point, faults we can find and judgements we can pass; but to what avail? It would not change the person or the result. With kindness, by example, by clearly expressing our wishes and maybe acknowledging some of their fears; by maybe letting them know how their imposing affects us, maybe just maybe we can make them aware of their actions, their words, their responsibilities and our boundaries. Obviously, it all depends on the scale of the situation, if severe enough, if all else fails we put in place one of the biggest boundaries of them all, we impart the lesson and we respect our boundaries by leaving. At a more mundane level of broken boundaries and not taking responsibilities however, as a fellow human being where would we all be, how would we learn and grow if each of us were ready to chuck in the towel at the first hurdle. The saying, 'once bitten twice shy' is a powerful one, but I personally believe that very often a clear word, just a genuine expression of feeling, presenting someone with a choice that they may have not seen or let sink in before, can make a difference to them as well as ourselves and our relationships, even if ultimately we choose to leave. Even the rule breaker, the boundary breaker the one that is afraid to admit and take on responsibilities, is trying to find happiness and a safe way home.

Chapter Thirteen

Lies

What compels a person to lie? It is a fact that we all have lied at some point or another and most of us still do. Whether it is a white lie, a small lie or a big lie, a lie is a lie. Also, what makes the distinctions between a small and a big lie? Where do we draw that line? Surely that is down to personal perspective. What is more hurtful, thus considered a bigger lie to me, might be of smaller significance to you. We often find ourselves saying "There was no need to lie", "Why did he/she lie to me?", "Can I trust him/her again?" What if instead of only looking on the outside for the answers to 'why the lie' we started looking at ourselves, what if we used ourselves as a starting point to understand this compulsion, this need to be untruthful. This way, not only we can get some perspective and understanding but we can also discover more about ourselves and the work required to raise ourselves higher and maybe set a precedent.

Leading by example, I know I have told white lies; and even these can have a different grading of size; protective lies, reassuring lies, lies to protect my backside for fear of the consequences and lies to keep people happy. I lied every time I told my children of the existence of Father Christmas, the Tooth Fairy, the Easter Bunny or anything that was to bring them that feeling of wonder and excitement. Then there where those times when I lied to them with the intent to protect them from situations which, in my opinion and understanding, I felt would bring them pain and a burden that was not for them to carry (whether because of their age or simply because I deemed it unnecessary for them to shoulder it, or because I felt it would rob them of their innocence or cause emotional turmoil); like all those times I shielded them from their father's fury and aggressive behaviour toward me and I stopped it escalating towards them. All those times that I rightly or wrongly (again it leans into a matter of opinion) that I covered up and justified their father's lies and behaviour in order to spare them from the emotional pain. Then there where those times where I lied to my mother, about smoking and having sex before marriage as well as those times when I told her I was working and instead I was with a friend that needed my support, but I knew my preferred choice would upset her. I lied to my employers all those times I was down in the dumps and suffering from depression and could not get myself into work; I lied to my friends all those times that I told them I was okay when I was really falling apart. Then, even more gravely, there are all those many times when I lied to myself, all those times I belittled and shrunk myself, all those times I told myself that I was not good enough and hid my head in the sand, kept myself stuck; all the lies I told and still tell myself every time I don't believe in me.

If I look closer into my lies and the reason for me choosing them over truth, it's fear; when we look deeper, we all lie out of fear. All lies are based on being fearful of something, whether it is the outcome, confrontation, disagreement, looking stupid, looking weak, being perceive as not being good enough, believing that that our opinion would make the other person feel bad and the list goes on. We all have to make snap judgements of what we deem best, in our interest as well as in the interest of those around us; and as a result of this, if we are honest to ourselves, we often find ourselves telling a lie. From this I deduce that the greater the fear the bigger the lie.

Some unfortunately, whether as a result of trauma, habit, learnt behaviour, narcissistic tendencies, or a constant state of fearful mindset get so used to telling lies that they turn their life into a total made up affair and who very often end up believing it themselves. To me this simply means that their need, their compulsion, their reasons to lie are simply greater than most.

I believe that no one sets out to lie with the pure intention of just lying, there is always a reason for hiding something. If we are bold enough and strong enough to believe in our actions in our intentions, then we would be honouring our truth and face the consequences that come as a result in those times that things don't pan out as we expected. In our healthy state, by seeing our choices as a way of growing and developing insight into ourselves and life, we are not afraid to speak the truth or the effect that this truth might have on us or those around us as we would accept that this is the path to understanding, self-discovery and enlightenment.

Many of us still have not opened our eyes to the fact that hiding behind a lie keeps us small, keeps us in the darkness, drama and confusion. Think about it, putting aside the lies we tell in order to surprise, and addressing instead all the other lies that stem from a fearful mindset, what happens when we lie? We worry about being found out, we feel guilty, we may even have to cover up our original lie and feed it even more till it finally becomes something that does not even resemble the little original lie. Then there is the fear of forgetting what you originally made up, and here if you are anything like me and have a memory like a sieve, then you really are in trouble! When we lie, we throw away so much energy, energy that if invested positively, would reshape and really enrich our life. Lying does not pay.

What many of us fail to realise is that when we learn to be truthful, when we dare to be ourselves and speak our truth regardless of the circumstances we best serve ourselves and others (what we might like to do is perhaps adjust the deliverance of our truth, it doesn't very often serve to be too blunt, not many people like to be hit with a verbal brick! A certain level of diplomacy and delicateness is generally better received). Being truthful to ourselves and others is a cleanser, it strips away the layers of mud we cower behind, we shield our true selves with. It deepens our courage to show our true selves, the courage to see and accept our imperfections as we learn and grow. It simplifies our lives, removing all those negative emotions and tensions that telling lies brings. Imagine yourself being free from all lies, telling them as well as maintaining them… did you just hear yourself taking a deep breath and feel your shoulders drop? The more you practice truthfulness the more you step away from the need to take over the responsibility of others' emotions, path and lessons; they don't belong to you. By developing this practice, you also learn to find yourself; facing more of who you are, bit by bit you remove the need to be someone you think you should be and slide into the person you actually are. You begin to accept and fall in love with the real you, warts and all.

A reason to love them - Having looked at ourselves, at our own lies and possible reasons for doing so; stepping away from that need to see our reasons for lying to be so different to the reasons of others, it might help us to see how love comes into play here.

Could it be possible that the reason other people lie seem different than ours is because we are at the receiving end of them and they hurt, they sting, and we don't like it? After all, it is not very often that we take the time to reverse the table as we tell our lies, well intentioned or not, to check, to see and feel the effect they would have on those who are at the receiving end if they did find out. Lies are a cover, we use them to cover up what we believe is not good about us, to be accepted, respected, liked and loved.

So, looking for a reason to love them I offer my humble perspective that the liars are people that are still in search of their own truth. They are simply struggling with owning themselves, their life and lack of self-acceptance. They, like us when we tell our own lies, are looking to find a way to validate themselves, their importance and their existence whilst at the same time fighting the fear of not being good enough. Maybe it might help this world if instead of throwing the book at them and shaming them, we helped them see their worth, letting them know, that we would have been able to handle the truth; teach them that we would have valued them more because of it. Promoting the message that helping and showing each other how to face the consequences, how to learn from displaying our courage and speaking our truth is more beneficial than shooting people down. Letting them know that most of the time, in reality, nothing bad happens, it is just what we visualise in our heads as a result, the mind reading we do, that causes us discomfort. Letting them know that, in fact, all is well and as it should be, and through them being truthful it's how those around them learn about themselves and grow. Reminding them that how others receive their truth is nothing to do with them.

Judgement does not change the lies; communication, understanding and living truthfully but setting an example, does.

Chapter Fourteen

Acceptance

Acceptance… Beside the general definition one finds in a dictionary, like many others, this word can have a different meaning for different people. For example, given the same scenario or situation, for some, acceptance may mean unconditional love with the willingness to take a person and their behaviour exactly for what it is; while for others it may mean resignation, giving into other people's ways, or even, 'letting them win'. Our perceptive of the same circumstances changes the meaning we associate to a word. We often believe we accept people for who they are, we even defiantly state, campaign even, on the importance acceptance has in our world, in our society, in our community. Overall, in a loose way, this belief we have of us being accepting does hold; however, if we look a little deeper, we might find that for most of us this acceptance might not run as deep or as true as we think. We very often are accepting of others as long as they are and do what we think they should be and should do. I came across a post on Facebook of late that depicted this down to a tee, it read: - Society: "be yourself". Society: "no not like that!". Our acceptance is conditional, i. e. I take you as my lawful wedded husband/wife, but I will try and change this or that about you because I don't like it or at least I think it should be done this way.

I would like to be clear, here, I am not talking about the compromising and adjustments that usually take place in any given interaction between people, in any type of relationship personal or impersonal; those are healthy willing adaptations which help relationships run smoother and strengthen the bond. I am also not suggesting in any way that the unconditional love type of acceptance does not have to hold any boundaries, on the contrary, healthy boundaries are a necessity for our well-being. The 'fake' acceptance, the conditional acceptance that I am addressing here and that we often fail to recognise, is the one that comes with a judgement and with a need to change another being. The acceptance that comes dressed as a wolf in sheep's clothing, the one that falls into criticising, and even extraditing someone because they don't conform with our way of being, living or understanding.

Lack of acceptance is often linked to our ego and/or to our need for perfection, obviously a perfection of our understanding. Although we might find ourselves often stating 'No one is perfect', with our non-accepting behaviour we send out a different message. Why is it so important to us that a person comes over to our way of thinking? Or, like in the movie Bridget Jones, someone should not fold their underpants because we don't. What makes our way right and theirs wrong? We say we are not, but every time we try to turn people over to our way of thinking, are we not sending out the subliminal message that our way is the right and perfect way? Then, looking on the other side of the coin, there is the big question, are we really not being accepted or is it all in our head? Are we in fact, projecting, on to the other person, our own lack of self-acceptance?

Many times in my life, I have not felt accepted. Without diving into the subject of full-blown rejection which we have already touched on, addressing more of a deeper, personal, family focussed emotional circumstance, the times I am going to draw upon here are of social relevance; friends and work orientated in nature. Linking into my book A Reason to Love Me, and the recount of those times when I returned home for the summer holidays from the convent school - when I joined the kids in my village on those Sunday afternoons playing volleyball and other games, many of them were very welcoming, others not so much so. I felt like the outsider, I felt inadequate, and in the eyes of those children that I felt they were not very welcoming, I felt unaccepted. Question is, was this the actual case? That was my feeling, my mind reading their behaviour and looks; it could have simply been that they struggled with newcomers and it was not, in actual fact, personal to me. Even if it was a case of not being accepted, would this really have any relevance toward me, or would it all have to do with the lens they were looking at my arrival with. Obviously, I did not have this insight at the time, but I now know that I did not have to feed my feeling of not being accepted. Whilst at the time I chose to use my energies to wear a mask and act like butter would not melt in my mouth, I could have chosen to use them instead to empowered myself by focussing on the power I had over this scenario; beginning with the acceptance of myself. Recognising the choices that were within my grasp. For example, I could have chosen to throw the mask away and focus on having fun, I could have chosen to focus and socialise more with those kids that made me feel welcome and accepted, I could have chosen to show my vulnerability and maybe more easily broken down the barriers with those who I felt showed resistance to my being there. I could have chosen to leave; I could have even chosen to find out if there really was a problem. The same could be said for my time at the school in the convent school, again, I felt the outsider when I joined in the groups with the girls that were not in the boarding school but were coming from the nearby village just for the lessons. Of course, some of the things they talked about I would have no idea of, as I was living a totally sheltered life, in a religious and world rejecting cocoon, a farfetched resemblance of what one would describe as a normal daily life family routine. Still, just because I felt I didn't fit in 'their world', it did not mean that I was not accepted. Sometimes we have to take a deeper look and see whether we really are not being accepted and when we just think we are not. There are the times however where things are immediately clear, and people make it understood that they do not want us in their circle, conversations, or company. This has happened to me a few times too, when people are prepared to accept you not as you are but with conditions. The people in this group are normally the more insecure people you will come across; they have to put the stamp of their power, of their importance, their views and they will choose carefully and vet anyone that falls onto their radar, allowing in only those that, in their mind, don't pose a threat or challenge to their validity and what they portray themselves as. An ex co-worker when I was working at a wine company wholesaler in my early twenties comes to mind here. She found any way possible to put me down, to keep me out of the team social banter in the office, as well as the out of office gatherings; for someone as sensitive and insecure as I was this was quite upsetting. It eventually transpired that she was seeing an Italian man, she was often showing off her Italian vocabulary and the knowledge she had of the Italian culture; so of course, me being Italian unnerved her and my presence was threatening to her social credence. She took it upon herself to believe I would judge any slip ups, and because of her self-consciousness, she chose not to *see me*, not to accept me, for who I really was but for who she thought I might be and pushed me out. My not being accepted was in fact her self-defence mechanism in action; she was simply fearful.

<u>A reason to love them</u> - A lot of the time whether we feel, or we actually are accepted or not, is a result of mindreading and miscommunication. We are part of a very intricate, multifaceted world, and a deeper insight into the other people or situations would greatly help in removing guess work and break down apparent barriers. There is a great quote that the writer and philosopher Thomas Cooley wrote which beautifully depicts my statement: - "I am not who you think I am; I am not who I think I am; I am who I think you think I am". This is true for most of us in any relationship we engage with whether personal or professional. Many of you may have also come across DISC, a behavioural assessment tool which helps to discern our personality traits and how-to best reach, understand and communicate with people according to these. To summarise it, there are four categories which result from this test: - D = Outgoing & Task; I = Outgoing & People; S = Reserved & People and finally C = Reserved & Task. Each one of these come with their own unique traits, and although most of us have some of the characteristics which appertain to each group, if we peel back the layers and go deeper into self-discovery we will find that we fall into one group more than the others. Although maybe not in full detail, this assessment tool is readily available online for anyone to try for themselves and is an interesting exercise to conduct. However, if you do try it, be mindful of the personal understanding of the given words, for example 'reserved' here, does not mean quiet and shy, you can still be the party girl/boy, be fully integrated and happily chit chatting with all; you are just not the life and soul of the party, the one that incites everyone onto the dance floor. Following this assessment, not only will it bring you self-awareness of how you work best, but if you pay close attention to those around you, their behaviour and communication, you will be able to see which group they fall into and therefore how to best reach them in their own 'language'. This learning makes a huge difference in our life and in other people in feeling accepted or rejected, understood, part of the group or made to feel like the outsider.

If we go to Italy and we ask for something in English, it's hardly surprising if the people we talk to will shut down and turn away from us leaving us with an information void. If, however we learnt to ask for that very thing in Italian, we would be met with a "Si, si…" and having been understood, we would get the information we need.

We often hear people saying 'treat people as you want to be treated' but adapting it to 'treat people like they need to be treated'- according to their personality needs, may give us better relationships.

There are often genuine times where we are not accepted by an individual or a group, those times where we have not misread any signals, or even if we have spoken to them in their 'language' they still put up a wall and have a resistance to our being. If you look deeper, you will find that this personality language still does apply. People simply see things from a different stand point, and sometimes they may not be emotionally as apt as the next person, or open to understanding, change, or someone new; it could even be as simple as you reminding them of a grumpy aunty in their childhood, in which case, you don't stand a chance from moment go. It is important to remember that people's inability to accept one person or a situation is a self-barrier a mastering of their own path not a reflection of you or the situation.

Acceptance like all other human 'needs' is subject to our own interpretation and our mirroring of our emotions onto others. Often it is according to our reading of the other person, our mood, our confidence or lack of, that we feel accepted or not accepted. The practice of 'coming back to us' here is very empowering. Focussing on our positive intention, on our path, on where we are going with regards to growth and life purpose, balanced with respect for all, with treating and speaking to others in their own language and their personality trait understanding, is all we are responsible for. The rest, in or out, does not belong to us.

With regards to us accepting people or situations, once we have done our best and right by ourselves and them, we have to remember that every season has its purpose. If it does not feel good, if it's not respectful, if it's hurtful, if it does not feel right, if it's not right for you, you don't have to accept it. Sometimes people learn to create a dialect in a language that others do not know how to speak. These people have built several layers of fears and self-protection and fighting battles that only they know. This is reason enough to love them even if it means us moving on.

Chapter Fifteen

Having A Voice

It has taken a long time for me to find my voice and to be honest, I am still working at it every day; to make it stand, to make it feel more comfortable, and every day I am getting better. You see, it does not come easy to me to make myself heard; having been shrunk and trained to make myself small does not allow for having a voice. It is a new practice for me, so some days it is just a whisper, on a few occasions it gets louder, when I talk about my passions it gets stronger and clearer. The biggest step I have taken in having a voice has been publishing *A Reason To Love Me*, where I stripped myself down to the very core and told the world all about my life. This did not come without its demons, fears and anxieties of possible backlash, which astonishingly never did come. In fact, as a surprise to me and my deep routed fears, I have been showered with amazing responses, and my intentions for writing it, which was to be of help to others on a much grander scale has worked wonders in its manifestation.

I have often been teased about becoming a UN ambassador. I've always been very good at bringing people together, at negotiating, at supporting, but I have never really taken a stand or taken a side. I have always rather preferred to find the positives in all sides and agree with them all. Actually, that's a lie. Although this statement is true for the majority of my life, I have not always been this way. I remember a very young me... she always took a stand, she always took a side, fearful she might have been, but she always spoke up; perhaps not so much for herself but she definitely used her voice to speak up for others.

You might say that with this book, by finding a reason to explain and understand 'the other side' I have not fallen away from my habitual 'UN ambassador' ways, but in fact, I have, I am actually exercising my voice. I felt from the very beginning that this book would be very controversial; I felt it would be especially grinding for the readers that might be fresh out of a situation where they have been wronged or damaged or may even still be in it. I knew when I decided to tell of my learnings and personal understanding that this may not be everyone's cup of tea and that to my 'horror', having spent my life wanting desperately to be loved by everybody, this may in fact make someone not like me very much at all, perhaps maybe even be angry with me for even suggesting a lot of what I have written here. Still, I chose to exercise my voice; taking a stand for my learning, my views and what I have come to believe. I felt a calling to write this book as I felt it would be those very people that would resist these ideas the most, that are in need of trying to work from a different perspective. Although no doubt thought provoking, these different perspectives that I have shared, that I am sharing, might be the cause of a spark, of something within which, if open to new idea, can help those very people overcome their pain, or make their life a little bit easier whilst navigating through their daily interactions, challenges, and looking at the conveyor belt of life scenarios and situations. Possible food for thought and maybe it warrants some time to reflect with a degree of honesty.

I have spent a lot of my life living by the idea that everyone else always knew better than me. I never felt confident enough or believed that my opinion would stand up to match those of others whom I always put on a pedestal and reputed as knowledgeable. I thought that if I disagree with others, not only would it make them not like me, but that it would hurt them, insult their superiority even (a status I always gave), and therefore make me a bad person. Many times I heard as the little me, that young girl that knew no limitations and believed in herself, being told 'you know nothing', 'stop being so pretentious', you are not to have an opinion', and even, 'be respectful and don't argue back'. These comments and many more like them, reinforced by derisory smirks, sentences and tuts which suggested how stupid, naïve, and unintelligent I was, took their toll and that little girl got silenced; she lost her voice.

This new belief grew stronger as days and months turned into years and despite the inner unrest and the resistance I felt at times, I forgot all about the girl that once had a voice.

It is only over the later years that I have come to discover more and more of me as I have learnt how to love me, as I have come to find my feet in the world that, through more and more whispering I have come to see my role, my importance, the fact that I too matter and that my voice matters too. This process has helped me to remember that little girl's self-belief and to readdress that belief that had been so radically changed. I now believe (although I might be whispering it here) that I, like you, are entitled to my opinion, that it is okay for me to speak and have a voice.

Although still at times faint, this new acceptance that I am entitled to have a voice and an opinion, has helped me with quashing a lot of my fears when it comes down to expressing myself (although making decisions is still not my point of strength... good thing with me, you would always get to choose where to go for lunch!). I now accept that it's okay for me to have a different opinion to other people and that it is okay for people to have a different opinion than mine; that this is simply due to a different interpretation and experiences in our lives. Although close, it is practically impossible for any two people to have precisely the same point of view down to each detail, the blueprint is different, so the view will be different. I have learnt that it is okay to disagree, it does not make one view better that another, just different. We don't have to take another opinion as our own, but it is important that each opinion is respected in its own right.

During my self-discovery, I have come to realise that I had formed the belief that if I was not validated by people, if people did not agree with me, this automatically would make me wrong, so except for the rare occasions where I tried to win them over to my way of thinking, more often than not, not wanting to seem stupid, and not wanting to be disliked, I clammed up and held my opinions deep within myself. With time however, through growth, study, hard work and practice, I have come to the magical understanding that I am not wrong, and surprisingly nor is the other person. In the moment of expression, both parties believe in their own opinion and, until either or both evolve to a different outlook, they are both valid. The amazing thing is that, while we share our opinions, learnings and point of views, if we are open to it, we spark within each other different 'light bulbs'. We take what we hear, we measure it against our beliefs, if we are brave enough we may even test it and try to apply it to our current situations and then we decide whether we reassess our thinking on that matter or if we deem our original view to be solid. This is how we develop, how we learn, how we grow.

A reason to love them - What can I say about the 'them' in here, there are so many people in so many sectors and circles in our lives who discourage and often ensure we refrain from having a voice. All of them guided by a fear of some sort. As children we have the adults in our lives that discourage us from having an opinion, a voice. When we are allowed to speak if it does not match our surrounding adults' opinion, we quickly get reprogrammed. We are told what we are allowed or not allowed to say and how to say it, and more often than not our truth gets quietened. It gets shoved so deep within a part of us that many of us spend the rest of our life gathering the courage to go find it and even longer in learning how to use it again. As we grow up and we step out from the confinement of our homes and its various associations, we have the input of teachers, neighbours, friends, bosses, colleagues, and all the sectors that as a society we have put in place to keep a 'fair' and 'safe' society: - The law, the courts, the political system, the police, the church, the media and so on. Whilst a lot of these are a much-needed guidance for our society, it is my belief the manner and extent to which their powers are being used have come to set us all into 'sheep mode' and fitting into boxes.

Do these people intentionally go out of their way to 'destroy' our unique curious beautiful selves? Do we in turn do the same to our children, to the young people in society, to the new generation, when it is our turn to be adults? Or is it a default formed out of a repetitive pattern which we have created and installed as a society over the many years that have preceded us? I feel the tight mode we work in as individuals and as a society is reflecting the fear spiral effect we live in; the more scared we get the tighter we hold on; the tighter we hold on the more fearful we get... and eat, sleep, repeat. A parent or guardian that shouts at a child not to argue back, may fear losing his authority, may question the validity of his opinion and his leadership as head of the family; he may even be afraid of being perceived by the outside world as a bad or unfit parent, so it tightens the reins. A teacher may not take the time to answer a student's question and tells them not to interrupt and get back to their books because he fears falling behind with his curriculum and not being seen as efficient or disciplined enough by his colleagues or the head of the school. A supervisor might not want to hear the reasoning of an employee that their computer crashed while completing a sale, his mind just jumps to the scary scenario of him not getting his monthly bonus and being unable to pay his mortgage, or perhaps he fears being questioned by the boss over his efficiency and position. A friend might distance himself after been presented with a different point of view because they may already feel so unworthy or unvalidated that they fear looking more into themselves and their truth. What each of these examples have in common is that the personal does not match the view of the masses. No one is really trying to intentionally hurt anyone, there is a confusion, a mismatch, an imbalance in our living that breeds and promotes fear. It seems that what we have created is a society that does not match our individual development, and the result of this imbalance is what we have come to depend on, rely on, and work by. It's fear. So, in fear we follow, we act, we agree, we lose our voices. It is difficult to stand up and be true to ourselves when we have been conditioned for so long and in so many aspects that if our opinion does not match the one of general society, it makes us different, it makes us trouble makers, it makes us outcasts, it makes us stand alone. When the majority of us are fed this message day in day out is it any wonder that people struggle to speak their truth, not only to others but also to themselves. This way the outer voice dies, often taking with it the inner one too, as it would only serve as a reminder of how painful it is to feel, to know, to express and not being able or allowed to do so; and so, we comply.

The perpetrators here have simply learnt the same 'laws' of survival and expressions we have.

Chapter Sixteen

The Balance of Give and Take

Some of us find the balance between giving and taking a bit of an issue. Again, through the learnings, examples given and the uniqueness of our travelled roads, some of us have learnt to tip the scales to giving and some of us tip it over to taking. When we stay closer to the middle, even if we lean more one way or another the effects and consequences are limited; but when we lean too much into either of the two and go closer to the extremes than the repercussions of being out of balance are strongly felt.

I for one have always struggled and found it difficult to take. To me taking has always come associated with a feeling of guilt and I have to overcompensate by giving twice as much to placate this uncomfortable feeling. Prioritising myself has been something I have come to learn and accept as healthy, and necessary, thus implementing it, over the latter part of my life. I was raised in a convent school which in conjunction with a very authoritative household, taught the unanimous message that one is not supposed to think anything of themselves never mind giving to oneself or receiving from another. I was raised with the message that I was not important enough, that only by being there for others I would deserve salvation, that it is only by prioritising and giving to others without receiving back that I would be considered good and one day I would get recognition for it and I could be 'someone' (In the nuns' opinion, that day would be when I died and would come face to face with God). On this basis, giving to myself or receiving, has never felt natural. I followed and lived by the rules and very clear messages of my teachers and focussed on only giving to others; becoming fully dependant on their lives, their thoughts and their opinions. My learnt behaviour has been primarily on serving others, but not in a healthy, humanitarian, purpose based or balanced way. I learnt to live only on one side of the scales, and on this topic, fully out of balance.

With time, experiences, study, and by meeting people that showed me a different outlook on the importance of give and take, one of them being my present husband, I have learnt to feel less uncomfortable by readdressing the scales. Don't get me wrong I still to this day feel the need for the scales to lean more to the giving, but I have learnt to accept to receive. One of the main things that worked for me was when someone (I cannot remember whether in person or in a book) reminded me of how good I felt when I gave to others and asked why I would take that feeling away from others by not reciprocating and allowing them to give. This for me was a 'life changing' moment, it opened a totally new point of view that made total sense and totally resonated with me. So, now when I go out with a friend for example, I won't insist and argue my way into paying every time (I always did this no matter how broke I was), instead I allow us to taking turns. Although I must confess, I still make sure that when I pay they get a little bit more than when they pay, keeping the scales a little tipped over to the giving; a little compromise I made with myself as I took on this journey of change in order to keep the 'demons', the encrypted guilt at bay.

What I now know, embrace and totally live by is a very different meaning of being of service to others than what I have been accustomed to believing; now noting and understanding the difference between being a servant and being of service. The service I practice now is not as a "I must", a job, a fear of punishment, or as a martyr; but one born out of love, compassion and care. One that is without condition and is for my benefit as much as for the benefit of others. In this practice I now also include myself, finally understanding that I am no less than another being, no second-class citizen as I have been taught to believe, but an equal, with my own gifts and importance. I also accept from others as I allow them to share their gifts, love and importance. Under this understanding I practice, request and insist more and more on the give and take. I also now understand, that only when I am happy I can share happiness, only when I feel love I can give love, when I have money I can practically enrich another's life, when I understand forgiveness that I can forgive; the list goes on. . . An empty vessel does not serve, a full one does.

The balance of giving and taking is paramount in any relationship, personal, interpersonal, in business and so on. If we only give and never take, never replenish, we empty. I have come to believe that although being of service (the healthy approach) is a major force in our development, in spreading our light and work as one, we are not giving our best when we leave ourselves behind; when we work from empty. In fact, when we always just give to others and don't let them reciprocate, this decision, conscious or unconscious, feeds our feelings of unworthiness as well as at some level, victimhood mode, can breathe resentment, anger and even jealousy; detachment and separation. The balance of give and take is not only important but necessary. It is important to maintain a healthy level of exchange that promotes growth, learning love, nurture, respect, and equality. Keeping a flow of positive energy flowing; working with the ebb and flow of life.

A reason to love them - Unlike myself, a person who has learnt to be and live on the extreme of giving, other people may have come to learn the very opposite and practice their living at the very edge of taking. This may be because they have experienced a lack of or have lived through painful experiences where they learnt to self-protect in this manner, or perhaps because the example and indoctrination of their teachers has been of this nature. Although many can be the reasons why some people could have come to practice the 'take' angle, I personally don't believe that they were born, as many people would label them, selfish or greedy. Besides our own blueprint, we all grow and develop from our experiences and the beliefs that are born from these. I believe that becoming defensive, judging, bitching and 'giving them a taste of their medicine' or cutting them out (and I have done this in the process of learning the balance), is not productive, helpful, kind or enlightening. How many of us run to our friends or family members and 'tell' on the taker instead of taking the bull by the horns and telling the person directly; explaining how this imbalance, their 'take only' mode makes us feel? Why not be that 'teacher' in their life that shows them a different way; the one that gives them a new perceptive. It goes without saying that this approach will work with some people, it might take longer for others to implement, and for others still, will not work at all as they might not be ready, willing, or are perhaps too afraid to step away from their known ways. As always common sense, sixth sense and any inner manual that keeps you true to your boundaries is to be followed and listened to for guidance. A point that might be of use here is to remember that your responsibility is always to plant the seed, but the outcome does not belong to you as it is dependent on the other person's path.

Here, I would like to offer some food for thought in the form of questions, as we can all be so harsh and be resentful of the takers, and often resist entertaining or understanding their actions or lack of. As I have said, for a long time I have lived as an 'extreme giver', and I have been commended for it on many occasions; if I look deeper however it begs the question... why is my 'extreme giver' worthy, getting me compliments and the 'extreme taker' getting slammed? Why does my approach make me a better person over the extreme of the taker? At the end of the day I too have chosen an extreme thus equally unhealthy. Also, as I mentioned, am I not as important as everyone else? This being the case, whilst I live in the extreme of giving, don't I continually take from me? On a humorous note, but hopefully one that drives home the point - at least the taker takes a bit from everyone, keeping it somewhat 'fair', I kept taking just from one person, me, until I sucked me dry.

As we learn and work to find the balance of the give and take in any field in our lives, it is important to remember I feel, that each of us is individual, unique, and we have unique gifts to share; it is only with the balance of give and take that we all get to show and share and benefit from these gifts. It is very important that we set and 'demand' balance, but it is also important that we find the balance in the setting and 'demand' in keeping with the timing of our learning. It is also essential to remember that just because someone is accustomed to taking, it does not mean that we have to comply and give; the power and the decision in our actions always does rest with us. We are the ones who teach others how to treat us. Perhaps, there is a double lesson for us givers every time we are faced with a taker; to learn to take and to teach to give.

Chapter Seventeen

The Importance of Caring for Self

Okay, on this subject I have a master's degree on how NOT to care for yourself, or at least I should have one! Caring for myself has never been a priority to me until I actually discovered some self-love, and that did not come into play in my life until a few years ago, over a decade ago now. If I could be unkind to myself, if I could have a go, hurt, punish, ridicule, belittle or use any other form of 'leaving me out in the cold' I would. This was not because I was a masochist or glad for punishment, this was as a result to my understanding that I was worthless, a message that directly, indirectly, deliberately or subliminally had been transmitted to me by those in a position of care during my childhood. I formed the belief that as not much care was taken toward me by those who presumably loved me, I was unlovable and thus unworthy of any care that was superfluous to the basic needs of food water and basic dressing. Not only I copied and self-applied the cold and practical human approach that was dished out as the norm during my growing up years, but I added to it other negative beliefs which I homed in on through my own interpretation. Beliefs of being insignificant, dispensable, and undeserving. On the basis of these negative views, I implemented their traits and behaviour in a much harsher way than they did, at times limiting and even denying myself of the basic needs. Interestingly, as I am writing a little light bulb just lit up in my head, and I can't help but wonder if that is where my need to be, at times, 'contradictory' partly comes from. To offer an example I remember an occasion while I was working for the previously mentioned wine merchant in London. As we were leaving one evening, one of my colleagues and a good friend passed a comment to me that I was getting too thin and was concerned, he knew only partly of my troubles at the time and I was not very forthcoming with many details, as I was always the listener, never the 'sharer'. A girl who was walking with us laughed at this and stated that men don't fall in love with bones they like meat; I recall thinking "good then I will have to lose some more weight".

Like many other good practices, the discipline of self-caring is for some of us something that comes with a lot of self-loathing; it is something that either for our own personal reasons we are adverse to and not used to, or we might take some sort of care but not with the need to nurture ourselves but with a view of entitlement.

With a few lessons learnt under my belt and having outlived the need and habit to self-persecute, I cannot emphasise enough the importance of taking care of ourselves. When we were children, granted, it was someone else's job and responsibility to take care of us and show us the ropes on how to do it; some, did a better job than others, still everyone did it to the best of their abilities and knowledge. As adults however, the buck stops with us. It is up to us to discover ourselves, to shed what doesn't feel good or right to us, to unearth our own beliefs, to try and err on the side of caution until we achieve the feel-good factor. It is our job to learn to extend to ourselves the love and care we are often quick to give to others in an attempt to make them feel good, to take away their pain, or to make them smile just because…

Like I tell my clients in their first session, you are born with you and you will die with you. Your mum may have given birth to you, but the journey into this world you took by yourself and when you die, you will no doubt have loved ones around you but the journey out of this world you will take alone. You are with you twenty-four-seven, everyone else comes and go; although all equal in the ladder of life and humanity, to you, you are number one. You need to learn to self-care, no matter how slow or quick the process, no matter how long it takes… it is not a race, it's a journey!

It is through the journey of self-discovery with our falls, scraped egos and, at times, tears that we learn to care for ourselves, that we fall in love with ourselves. If we pay attention, we are guided all the time, our childhood carers were not the only ones with guidance, information and examples on the 'how to'. Every day we encounter people from all walks of life and they too are our teachers, in fact, every single one of them is our teacher whether it is helping us to form our beliefs on 'how to' or on the 'how not to'. So, there are no excuses, we are responsible for our lives, and the sooner we embrace this responsibility the sooner we can start living our way, and to live at our best we need to master the art of looking after and taking care of ourselves in mind body and spirit.

Starting with the mind… learning to take care of the mind has been a very long, challenging but intriguing and exciting journey for me. I had to learn first-hand, never mind the books, what I now 'teach' and share with my clients. I had to learn how to change my inner communication, to talk nicer to myself, in my case to become my friend instead of my worst enemy. I had to learn how to be gentler, to be compassionate instead of always on the attack and constantly having a pop at myself for one thing or another. I had to learn how to look at the opposite side of the darkness, a view which I was very well accustomed to see from; and see instead from the light perspective. I had to learn to truly commit to 'see' me, not from the version that had been passed down and shown to me by the adults in my childhood, well-meaning or otherwise; but from point zero, no perception, just curiosity, determination, perseverance and daily work. No matter how fed up and frustrated or stuck I felt, I tried and kept trying until I found what worked for me. I implemented various techniques: -

Giving Thanks, Affirmations, Positive Visualizations, reading Self-help material, the practice of Changing Negative Thoughts into Positive ones, and the STOP technique, just to mention a few. These practices, piece by piece brought me to own a very different mindset one that seemed and felt truer and like home to me. They helped me with my self-discovery, to get to know the real me, how I function, what makes me tick, whilst living a happier life in a much stronger yet lighter, and positive mindset.

With regards to the body I have to admit that I haven't been a good ambassador for taking good care of mine, I have starved it, and I have fed it (and often still do) the less nutritious of foods. Over the years, in fact, from childhood, I have consumed way more than my fair share of alcohol and junk foods; I have judged it, I have hit it and hurt it. I am mesmerised by my younger son; he is very respectful of his body he takes good care of himself. It obviously does help that he has an extremely caring mum who despite of her own failings has taught him his worth ;-). Coming back down from my pedestal, he does get the fact that our body is in fact our temple, it is our vessel to experience this life, if we don't take care of it, we cannot experience this life in the best form and chance we have been given. Remember there is only one of you, you matter; and although the focus is on our experiences, our progress, our growth, our journey, our body matters; good health is a gift and the least we can do is maintain it by taking good care of ourselves.

Lastly taking care of our Spirit. This one is possibly going to be the most personal and individual aspect of the three, although the mind and body may differ in perspective and experience from person to person, as an 'abstract' an 'unseen', Spirit is arguably even more multi-layered and faceted; and as such everyone has many different layers in views and opinions. It carries a 'wider' meaning and is open to a multitude of understanding, feelings, interpretations, beliefs and emotions. Whichever the individual interpretation and meaning of Spirit, whether you perceive it to be an external force or you be It or both, Spirit carries with it a sense of trust, hope, reverence, power, force and limitless expression which no man can fully comprehend. It is a drive, a source, that although we all try, it is intangible and impossible to put 'Its' wholeness into words. No matter how clear we feel and believe we are about Spirit it always retains a sense of mystery, of wonder, of more…

No matter what the understanding of Spirit, its 'function' is the same for us all; between the many and the ones I have already mentioned, is to keep us dreaming, faithful, believing and trustful in our journey. How to take care of the Spirit side of us? Well, we all have our own ways, rituals, routines even. Whatever it is that we use to keep our flame alive – whether it is prayer, setting intentions, meditation, visualization, singing or reading, it is important to practice it regularly. Repetition shapes the way and sets the mould; it depicts our path.

A reason to love them - Here I could write about the perpetrators as being those people who, when we were young, did not teach us the importance of self-care and that perhaps, did not give us the techniques to implement it so that we could tend to ourselves in the best way possible. But, if it is true that we can find a silver lining in everything, how can we ascertain that their teaching was not of use to us in this sense? Is it possible that what they did share with us was simply what they felt was more in line with their understanding of self-care? For my mum might it have been my appearance, my look; my father's obsession with enforcing impeccable reputation and always pleasing others could have been a form of self-care so as to avoid emotional bullying and confrontation; the nuns in the convent school by installing the fear of God into me, might have thought they were teaching me self-care in the way of protecting myself from what they believe to be evil.

Given that we are all different and unique, caring and our perception of it will differ. We might feel we have been hard done by, but it may simply be that our ideas and meaning of things just matches a different image in our head than that of others. For example, whilst the self-care I was taught from my parents focussed on my dealings with the outside world, my own perception of self-care is more of an inside job, it is inner dependant, so their actions or words were never going to match with my view.

For this, I once again call upon the self and make it accountable for how we treat ourselves. Although easy to point a finger and pass the blame as I mentioned, throughout our lives we do have many influences, we cross paths with many people, showing us many different options; and it is up to us what we choose to learn and apply. I am going to digress a little here and give an example of the different views where one can perceive it as inadequate and another can see it as purposeful through lessons that are put in our paths. I am going to share a situation which was brought to light after I was attacked and has shone a different light onto my upbringing. I, as well as most people that know of my childhood and how I was raised, have at first glance, come to describe it as harsh, cold, unloving and other not very positive words. To make use of judgement, perhaps an 'unfair' childhood, where parents should have known and done better. What if I told you that, that very same upbringing could be seen as being exactly what I needed to grow my strength and be able to save my life in years to come? After the attack in my flat in London and following the case that was splattered all over the news and newspapers, several people wrote to one of these newspapers asking them to pass on their cards and letters to me. One of the letters was from a family who had moved to France. In this letter following their expression of sorrow for my endurance and their kind offer of opening their house to me if I ever needed to get away, there was something else. They congratulated my parents for raising such a strong woman. Whilst at the time that comment stung as I felt they too were taking my power and the recognition for my survival away for me, once away from the immediate trauma, I was able to see the gem and the lesson I was to take from that sentence. For this I will always be forever grateful to them.

So, resuming… yes, during our earlier years we absorb and form strong beliefs which run as an undercurrent in the back of our mind at every opportunity, like an inbuilt memory card in a computer, a blueprint which we refer back to and measure by. However, many are the teachings available nowadays for our evolvement and restructuring of that inner program, that inner map, that does not justify our idleness in growing through ways that are any less than good for ourselves. So here the perpetrators, I would like to name are ourselves. The good thing is, I am not going to find anything but understanding for those of us who have behaved less than nice or caring toward ourselves. Life is not a race but an amazing learning opportunity, dependent on our path, our own unique pace and way. A lesson that someone may have learnt at the age of ten might be learnt by someone else at the age of sixty, all is relevant to our path, surroundings, opportunities and life purpose that we are here to experience; no comparison, no winners or losers. We all take care of ourselves in our own way. Just because some of us have learnt to do it in a less than kind way, in a way where we might even self-destruct, does not mean we are stuck with it. As we learn to do better, we do better. Different paths, different ways, different perceptions, different ways to self-care; for some of us the dots that join self-care and self-love don't come until later in life, but that does not mean we don't at some level self-care, just not in a way that might be considered more socially acceptable. If you feel that someone's way of self-caring may not be the best, by all means show them a different way, but never judge them, criticise them or impose, they are simply acting on what they know; we all do the best we can with what we have.

Chapter Eighteen

Letting Go

I don't know about you but letting go for me is one of those 'Mmmmm' moments. Here I am referring to the practical, physical letting go; the letting go in action. Not only I am not best at choosing and making decisions overall, but I always resort to "one more try", "Let's give it one more week" and "I have to try everything, so I don't have any regrets" inner chatter. Question is… when is that last try, that last week? How do we know when we have tried everything? We run away with our thoughts, we scan our life scenarios and those of the people that we count as relevant for the current circumstances and try to come up with more ways that give us a reason not to let go, to keep the status quo. Like me you might have formed a belief that giving it your all, being the sensible, 'serious', committed one, even at the cost of being a martyr, makes you a good and righteous person. Using relationships as an example, I have on many occasions found myself playing in my head a sentence that I have heard time and time again "all is fixable, people just don't work at things anymore". The dread that I would be seen as a quitter, that I could be seen to be getting things wrong, that I would be 'that one' that disobeyed the rules of the older 'wiser' generations has caused me to feel stuck and trapped more times that I can remember, throughout my life experiences. We often forget that having the courage to let go and on the other side of the coin, keep holding on, is the product of our thinking, our beliefs, the stories we tell ourselves. There is a line between quitting and giving things your best shot. Every situation is unique and what really helps is the ability to be honest with ourselves. For example, are we holding on out of fear? Are we holding on because is easier? Are we holding on because in doing otherwise we would see ourselves as failures? Or, are we holding on because we truly feel in our heart better times are coming, because we really feel it is the right thing to do or perhaps because we feel and believe that the situation or relationship is the real deal and the troubled time is just a hiccup that helps us grow stronger and closer together. When we follow the feelings, those gut feelings, instead of the thinking process; when we follow unconditional love, the trust in the bigger picture, in the process, then things become a little bit clearer. The very first thing it is good to let go of, are those very beliefs, that very thinking that's holding us back and keeps us living in fear. The belief I have shared at the beginning of this chapter for example, it is not even my own belief, not something of my creation, just something I have adopted from my family and culture from a very young age. My inability to let go of this belief has made for a very troubled life. Because of this belief (as well as others just as unhelpful), I dragged out relationships that if I had instead removed swiftly like you do a plaster, I would have saved myself a lot of time, pain and heartache in exchange for more confidence, self-love, self-esteem and self-trust. A life where maybe the scales would have mirrored a more favourable balance on its happy/miserable setting.

Recalling the experience of my relationship with Alex from my first book, my need to hold on, the not wanting to let go even when all the signs were there that the lessons had been learnt and the relationship had run its course. My unwillingness to let go and his need for emotional power, made for too many 'unneeded', and very painful years. Although I have no doubt in the love that I felt for him, we were coming from a very different place, very different paths and had very different dreams. Looking back, if I was practicing unconditional love and trusted more in myself and life, I would not have held on so tight and inflicted on myself so much pain. However, at that time I had not yet learnt, never mind let it sink in, that I could have chosen my gut feeling, my inner knowing over my fearful thoughts, and those restrictive beliefs. So, despite how loud my inner voice was shouting within me, I let the thoughts and fears run wild and kept firmly in line with the old and strongly practiced ways. As the vulnerable girl I was then, driven by negative beliefs, fears and lack of identity, I chose to focus on all the thoughts that would give me an excuse to hold on, focussing on all those things I could hear, in my head, my parents and other 'significant' adults say: - "you are a screw up, you can't make anything work", "you got pregnant with this man and had an abortion', no one else will ever want you", "you introduced a black man into our home, ridiculed us in front of our community, you have to stay with him now", and one more, "you made a horrendous mistake by having an abortion, now you have to make this work so you can get married and have a legitimate child with him; your pain will go away and your father won't kill you". None of these were good reasons to stay and force a relationship into play, and this thinking did certainly not come from a place of what was best for me or him. So, I crawled and begged and allowed all sorts of maltreatment, it did not help that I had no self-esteem, self-worth or love for myself. With this refusal to let go, at that time under the false flag of "but I love him so much and love conquers all", through actions and reactions, we just brought the worst out of one another, a vicious circle, fighting a lost battle, trying to save what was no longer meant to be. This resistance to let go in the end took us to a place of no return; so much pain (at least on my part) which a more pure and wiser loving heart would have avoided. My soul knew – my human side refused to listen.

In order to best recognise when to let go is to first learn to listen to ourselves. Not to that part that scans every life experience we have been through, the analytical mind the adding and subtracting and the solving of equations; nor the irrational emotional reactive part of ourselves. We need to learn to trust ourselves, to develop our inner knowing, to get to 'see' from a 'what is the lesson' point of view. "How does this serve me and others? Is this from ego or love? What is the bigger picture? And maybe more importantly we have to balance out pain and happiness, something that hurts us more than makes us happy is telling us that we are off course.

Looking at letting go from another major angle, is to learn to let go mentally and emotionally. We are all so good at holding on to memories and emotions that, although no longer in existence, we give them a huge amount of power and energy. Many of us struggle with forgiveness, despite the situation ending weeks, months or even years ago, we relive it in our head time and time again. This is the most vicious form of self-abuse. With this practice we hurt ourselves, we poison our bodies, we tear down our current relationships and dealings; we become blind to our daily gifts and opportunities. The best present we can give ourselves is the permission to let go; to accept and understand that any past situation, no matter how bad and painful, is over and done with. Not one single thing can be changed from what occurred, not one smidgeon of thought, anger or vengeance can take it away or alter it. The ability of letting go of grudges is a gift that keeps on giving as it frees us from further pain and the resulting unhappy living that would come from the manifestation of that thinking.

<u>A reason to love them</u> - Given the two points I have chosen to discuss in this chapter of 'Letting go', I am going to address as the perpetrators, our beliefs for the first part, and those who have caused us to feel aggrieved for the second part.

Our beliefs, for all their 'wrong' doing at times, have been created and absorbed by us for a reason. Call it lessons, direction, path or purpose. It is through living out our beliefs that we experience life and it is through the arranging and rearranging of them, that we grow, discover and find ourselves. So, to wrap up the first point in understanding and give love to beliefs as perpetrators, it is my opinion that whatever the reason we have come to believe something, and take it on as a personal belief (even when we discover it to be non-beneficial), it served a purpose. It was for a reason, an agenda, a part that served us to evolve, and fit into a bigger picture. Again, nothing is wasted or in vain.

As for the second part, those who have caused us to feel aggrieved, in their blueprint and learnt world they would have been simply following their own beliefs and their understanding of life. These people are not our enemies, they are not on a personal mission against us. They may or may not realise the pain, angst and at times destruction they have activated within our lives. What is important is to understand that the power over our lives does not rest with them, their words or actions towards us; it rests with us. We can look at them as intentional aggressors and pain givers and get trapped on the 'whys' and 'I wish' spiral of thinking, or at their role in shaping us into the warriors we are and use those events and experiences to focus on understanding and recognising our greatness. I will go more into this in the chapter 'My Assailant', but for now let me just remind you that in order to grow, experience this life and find our purpose, all colours of causes are needed to help us find our way.

Chapter Nineteen

My Assailant (and Forgiveness)

Some of you might have felt that in this book I have 'justified' or excused the perpetrators and some of you who have read my first book might even wonder how I am going to relate the world love to someone who has caused me so much damage and took me so close to death; namely my attacker. For those of you who have not read my first book, in my twenties, whilst living in London, a schizophrenic who had recently being released from Broadmoor broke into my home raped me several times at knife point and, had I not managed to (eventually) escape, would have killed me to raise his profile when he got back to prison.

You will find that there is probably more content to this chapter than in the previous ones. This is not because in my eyes it holds more value or I deem it to be of greater importance, but simply because, following on from the enquiries and subsequent conversations which followed my first book, it seems to be the one situation people found the most difficult to understand and accept my applying of love and forgiveness.

I myself have struggled with this one the most, relating the world love to this man, made the whole of my body and skin crawl. However, that was because when I thought of this person, awful images filled my mind in association. I noticed, and this awareness is what eventually made a difference in my means to overcoming this barrier, that if I related the world love to the man and the images he provoked in my head, it made it incomprehensible and totally unconceivable for me to have any reason to have love for him (even as I type aligned with this thinking, I can feel the resistance). BUT, if I looked at the soul of this person, the purpose behind, the lessons, the journey which each of us are here to experience in order to become who we need to become, and the intricate exchanges each path imparts in the tapestry of life, my perceptive changed. A deeper understanding developed, and with it came peace.

So, I am just going to dive into it…

"Why do people hurt people?" is a question that is at the forefront of most of our minds when a horrendous act takes place. The answer that often seems to surface is "Hurt people hurt people".

On a radio interview when I said I had forgiven my attacker I was met with shock and disbelief, after all not only did he do what he did to me, but he was out to take my life. My reason for it then, and still is now, is that I believe that no one is born bad; we are either ill or we have learnt the behaviour. With regards to the first one we need to address the illness and for the latter we need to 'retrain', offer the offending party a different perspective. One of the callers even said that I owed it to other victims NOT to forgive him. My question here would be "Why?" To be an example of living pain? To teach others how to self-destruct perhaps. . . because that is exactly what would happen, I know, I've tried it. How would this hate, or anger help me or anyone else? Another radio presenter asked me the question "What if he doesn't want your forgiveness? Who cares! Forgiveness is not about the other person, forgiveness is not justifying the other person's behaviour, forgiveness is about us, it's about letting go of the anger and hate that would otherwise consume us. Forgiveness is about giving ourselves permission to stop pressing the replay button of a time that no longer is and choosing to live our life our way, in this moment. Let's face it, I could choose to spend a lot of my energy focussing on the negative events in my life, on those people that were the catalysts in those events, my ex-husband, my ex-boyfriend, my father and above all my attacker; any person who I feel has done me wrong. Perhaps even focus on how karma should pay them a visit and let them feel the pain I felt… but that would not serve me. In choosing the road that I have chosen, in choosing to let go, to free myself from a need to change a past that cannot be changed, to let go of the need for revenge, is a gift that keeps on giving. Someone's disconnection does not have to ruin our lives; we can choose not to give it permission to do so. When we choose to hold on and be angry, hold grudges or hate, we only hurt ourselves;

the other person is not even aware of how we feel. The saying 'hate is like drinking poison and expecting the other person to die' is very true, these negative emotions harm only us. Although the attack happened many years ago, if I keep that memory alive through hate and anger the effects on my mind, body and spirit would be as detrimental today. As a result of trauma by getting stuck in repetitions of hurtful thoughts and images, we keep ourselves stuck in 'victim' mode; this addictive mindset serves to prolong and intensify our pain. With all this emotional turmoil we find ourselves placing the blame and keeping the focus solely on the event itself, thus keeping us under the illusion that we are powerless and that our lives are ruined forever. This could not be further from the truth. Our lives can resume at the very moment we take our power back, when we remind ourselves that our life belongs to us; that it is us who shapes this moment NOT a memory, NOT another's actions, NOT someone else's interpretation of life.

Don't get me wrong, this understanding did not come to me over night. After the event occurred, I spent a lot of time hating him, wishing him the worst of the worst. I was in pain, I felt and thought of myself, as a victim. I felt trapped, hard done by; the pain, the anger, the hate consumed me. I wanted payback. Then I slithered, crawled, walked… all the time moving forward returning the focus back to me, to the one and only who actually has any control and say over my life, me. It took me a long time to appreciate that this event, although a horrific experience at the time, brought with it so many gems, so many lessons learnt; all filtering through at different times, dropping in as I grew and when I was ready to recognise them. We can't rush our way to healing; healing is personal and path dependent.

I have done a lot of work around healing and forgiveness in order to comeback to a state of inner peace, after all life has presented me with plenty of situations to practice with. The fact that I have chosen to forgive him and the way I have come to support this forgiveness has been understood or at the very least accepted by most people who I have had the pleasure to work with (through all the various ramifications of my business), and those I have engaged in conversation with on this matter. The minority that still find it incomprehensible, unacceptable and therefore reject the idea, have generally drawn this conclusion based on the fact that the person is either still in the earlier stage of the process of healing, or they themselves have not been in such severe and intense situations, and therefore cannot quite comprehend the immense reward (or the work and thinking that it involves), to achieve this state of overcoming and freedom. It has been a long journey to recovery, understanding, learning, life ownership, forgiveness, and emotional freedom. I have worked hard to come to own this new perspective, but life has slowly but surely guided me to it, and the release of that weight off my shoulders has been so refreshing, inspirational and uplifting. In life we can choose to take responsibility or place blame. On my way, on the road I have travelled, I have come to understand that we are each a star in our own movie, this movie that is our life… and every one of us are in turn each other's supporting act (including the 'bad' guy; every movie has a 'bad' guy! No one wants that part, but someone's got to play it). An intricate web of imparting and receiving lessons as we all play our roles… all doing the very best we can in finding our own way, with the lines we have come to learn and the music we have come to hear. With this understanding there can be no place for blame, anger or hate; only acceptance forgiveness and love.

It takes all sorts in this world in order to impart each other's lessons. For a start I have learnt that nothing is for nothing, everything is for a reason, we learn, we grow, we discover ourselves and our power, through the lessons we find life. Perhaps the most important lesson I have learnt at the hands of this man, as well as other disturbing times in my life, is that I am stronger than I ever realised. I have learnt that **I am what is left when all is gone**.

Other questions we ask ourselves when we feel hurt by another's actions or behaviour are "Why me?" or "Why did he/she do that to me?" I found that it helps to change our perspective when we come to answer these questions. Instead of taking the stance that life or people are out to get us, it helps to switch the focus to "What is my lesson here? What is this telling me?", "How can this serve me? How can I use this lesson?" We only to often focus on the cause rather than the solution; the cause keeps us stuck the solution moves us forward. In the first instance we relinquish our power, on the second we take our power back. When we look at things from the perspective of growth, pathways, understanding and vision, we are less likely to fall into victimhood and more into warrior mode.

Another point of focus I found keeps me in my state of peace, is to remind myself of our individuality, the unique understanding we have come to own during our journey, and our purpose. We can only view any given situation as a result of these factors, thus assess each given matter from this perspective and behave in accordance with it. A simple analogy I like to keep at the forefront of my mind when my head regresses to the old pattern of stepping into anger, blame or upset over someone else's behaviour which I might find hurtful or unacceptable, is the analogy of the 6 and the 9; depends on which side of the number you stand you will read it one way or the other.

We all have a different point of view of each given situation and life, people can only see things from their point of understanding and their interpretation of life. The man who attacked me will not understand my message that what he did was wrong because in his eyes, through his illness, his lessons learnt, and the path he has walked, what he did, to him is 'normal' behaviour. No matter how many times I could tell him it's wrong, he would laugh at me and tell me it's right.

<u>A reason to love them</u> - There are different roads I could go down to offer reasons to love people like my assailant. For a start I could go down the road of the law of attraction where it states that we are fully responsible for everything and everyone that we attract into our lives. However as I feel that I have already 'pushed my luck' with some of the opinions I have offered and shared in this book, I am going to steer clear of this angle on this occasion and stick to personalities, perspectives, paths and a small drop of spirituality.

I know very little of this man's life, except for the bits that have slipped from the mouths of those in one position or another, who assumed I knew about his past. Again, I am not here to justify but to 'report' and keep to facts. I will not divulge details of his life, as his life story is his own and for him to disclose if he ever chooses. To give a general outlook, he has multiple conditions under the umbrella of severe mental illness, as well as, to put it mildly, his childhood was not one from which any child would come out of unscarred.

Going back to where I have already touched upon, this confirms the answer I gave at one of the radio interviews I was invited to; we are either born ill or we learn the behaviour. In my attacker's case both apply. Each one of us can do our best with what we have come to learn in each given moment then when we know better (and in his case unfortunately that better never seems to have come), we do better.

Something I would like you to ask yourself: - If an animal is ill or in pain, and as you tend to him, fearful of your touch, he bites you, would you hold it against him? Would you be angry at him, resent him, or even hate him and never forgive him for it? Chances are you may be wary of going close to him in future. When you approach him again, the image of that event may flash through your mind and make your approach more tentative and you may feel fearful of the new moment, as self-preservation and self-protection kick in; but I dare say, you would not hold ill feelings against him. So why hold resentment, hate or anger toward a person who has wronged us or hurt us? Behind every ill action or words there is a hidden pain, fear or illness that the giver is dealing with, and the recipient is not aware of. You may say "Yes, but killers, rapists and those who cause the most vicious of acts are different!" My response to you here is one of challenge by questioning, by yet again, thought provoking questioning... How can we justify one and judge another by the outcome, when the underlining reasoning and drive is the same? Does the level of severity of the lessons a person has learnt, or the severity of their illness make someone a bit bad or very bad? Or, is a lesson learnt or an illness, regardless of the severity, still a lesson learnt and an illness to correct and cure? If your child or your parent or best friend or brother or sister were the result of bad lessons, maltreatment or suffered from severe mental illness, would you rather have them lynched, killed even, or corrected and cured?

It is my belief that we cannot change a hurt, hateful heart by meeting it with more hurt and hate, but rather, with love. Remember an eye for an eye makes for a blind world; meeting hate with hate will only serve to spread its fire. Everyone wants to be loved, and although they might resist it at first, I have found that sooner or later most will meet you with it.

I know this is a hard one to process and it might take some time to digest; for some of you the response to my suggestions here might even be an indignant one and one of total outrage. I totally understand if this is the case, it took me a long time to step away from the condemnation that sat in my heart as a result of the attack. It took a lot of work and self-healing for me to come and rest in the peace in which owning this more compassionate outlook has brought me to.

As I said at the very beginning of this book, all I offer is a different perspective, a thought-provoking perspective; food for thoughts. I just hope that, although you may not resonate with, never mind embrace the ideas I have just presented, you simply allow yourself to consider this different view. As again, it is not meant to justify the perpetrator's behaviour, but to help you step back into your peace; away from fear, away from the anger that would otherwise consume you. When we hate we hold on; when we forgive, we let go. We set ourselves free.

To End...

For those of you who have read 'A Reason to Love Me', hopefully, you would have found this, an equally 'interesting' read, as it offers an insight, a link into how I have come to view life in this manner. To see the connection between those experiences circumstances and events I have lived through; and how much this new perspective has come to bring me peace and allow me to live a much more tranquil life.

I appreciate that this book, for many, will be a controversial book, they maybe even resent me for my suggestions. Whilst the first reaction might be to shut down to these suggestions and perhaps even run away with your mind to forge an immediate argument against each and every given point, I would love it if even just for a little while you entertained the ideas I offered, as I found them to be miracle workers in my process of healing. It might be a controversial book, but I believe it is so because it offers a perspective which is not promoted in the media or in our society overall. It is a book for those that choose not, to keep a close mind and barriers up, but who opt to try, to open themselves up to a different perspective; a different point of view to healing and growth. A point of view which has freed me from (most of, as I too, am a work in progress) the chains of a very destructive past.

We can all use the Freudian approach and look for the root cause of our problems, our pain, why we behave in a certain way, and who we have come to be. However, the cause without the courage of action does not bring about change. Once we come to have our answers, the choice that follows dictates whether we live our lives through happiness and freedom or through struggle and entrapment. If after our root cause discovery we use it to blame and focus solely on that event, person or situation we become stuck in painful negative emotions; every time we get entangled in blame we give our power away, we stop looking for solutions believing that our happiness is in someone else's hands. Believing that unless they fix it, apologise, or change, there is nothing we can do, as after all it's their fault. We enter victim mode. If, however, after founding our reason for the 'why' we follow up with the Adlerian approach, and we use that past, those circumstances, as allies, as tools, as an asset, we can use them to shape this moment. This approach spurs us toward action, solutions, and growth. Looking at our past with the view to learn rather than to judge and play victims, encourage us to take our power back, evolve, develop, discover ourselves, our power and create the life we want. With this mindset, we are no longer victims but masters of our world, our own destiny. No longer waiting to be rescued or swimming in doom but reliant on the safety of our own power, abilities and strength.

Some of us will repeat our 'teachers' pattern, some of us will go on to be the complete opposite, and some of us will find the balance. All for a common purpose: - GROWTH. In order to grow we need different experiences, understanding, people with different beliefs, ideas and behaviour; even if we sometimes strongly disagree with them. Keeping in mind that it is never the situation, words, action or person that makes us feel one way or another but our view and interpretation of it.

As I have said, 'A Reason to Love Them', is not an argument to justify, but to understand another's behaviour and our interaction in relation to it; with a view to return the focus and power to ourselves by choosing a different outlook. Perhaps to help release the anger, guilt, fear, sadness, burden that we have been carrying with us for far too long and was never ours to carry, thus allowing us to lead a more peaceful life.

I would like to make it clear, that whilst I do promote understanding and compassion, I am a flag bearer for safety and living life to the full. Just because we come to understand the actions of another's behaviour, we do not have to endure it (I have come to 'understand' the actions of my attacker and learnt to have compassion, but would I have him over for dinner? I think not!). If at any time you find yourself with anyone, or in any situation that does not serve you or that causes you harm of any form, I urge you to safely put a distance between you and the person or situation, because life is for living in the most enriching way, whatever that way is for each of us.

To reiterate, I have written this book with the aim to guide your focus towards the good and even the beauty that can be found in people and situations, in life, regardless of how difficult they may appear to be; not to validate them, but to support you. To look through the eyes of curiosity, looking to find the 'gems' instead of the problems that any interaction with a particular person, or your involvement in a particular situation is offering you. To see those, who you perceive as perpetrators not as enemies, someone to fix, rescue, judge, an obstacle, or even a mean to hold yourself back; but simply as someone unique in their own way, flaws and all. Someone with an understanding of life and living that is different than yours, still doing the very best they can with what they have come to believe. Remembering at all times the power you truly hold, that if they are someone you like and somehow fit with, you stay and you deal with it; or if not, you accept them for who they are and simply and freely choose to walk away. Remembering that, loving them sometimes means leaving them because sometimes it is only when we do that, that we allow them to see the lessons; to see that the way they do things doesn't work and they need to find a different approach.

Your life is yours, don't complicate it with drama and despair, treat it as discovering new ground, a crossword puzzle to find the answer to, that reveals more and more of you and the amazing being you are. Life moves forward, it's up to you whether you choose to spend it by giving your power away, angry blaming or seething over a past that is gone, or in peace, self-fulfilment, laughter and owning your journey. Time waits for no man, anyone or anything! I know the me now chooses to stay in my peace, joy and in my living, over drama and hurtful memories. Reminding myself that living is in this moment in action not stepping into thinking and reminiscing, as thoughts are just imagination at play. If I choose to step into thinking I'd much rather make it an enjoyable one and daydream about nice things. Don't get me wrong, I too as much as the next person have fearful and often negative thoughts that crop up as well as scary images from my past, but when that happens, as soon as I become aware, I make it a point to stop entertaining it and direct my thinking onto something pleasurable. The practice of this technique has helped to limit the amount of darkness in my mind and more often than not, keeps me in a positive mindset. I practice living in the now, to be present with the people in my life, so that I don't miss all the special moments that take place; moments that stepping into thinking would rob me of.

As a final thought, I'd like to offer a reminder that we always have a choice. Every moment we get to choose how we feel by selecting our thoughts; we are only ever one thought away from a feeling of OKAY. It is only when we engage with our thoughts, via a negative interpretation of the event that we enter fear, pain, depression, and anxiety. By readdressing that thought, or even better, by staying in the moment, we step back into peace, we take our power back. In this very moment, away from thinking, wishing or reminiscing, we are okay. Thinking is completely different to living.

The experiences in our lives do not define us; the way we look at things, the way we interpret those events, and the power we choose to give to those experiences (and people who were part of them), are at the base of how we live and experience life now.

When we focus less on the mistakes, on faults and judgement and focus more on our living, our life gets easier, we become happier; as the focus goes not on what we can't control, paths and lessons that don't belong to us, but on where we are, what we choose to do with each moment at hand and where we would like to go.

At the end of the day the root of the matter is, the only expectations we need to have is of ourselves (in a loving, gentle and compassionate manner), so to grow, improve and become each day a better version of ourselves; no comparing, no demanding, as although we are part of a whole, and therefore here to experience interpersonal relationships, our experience starts with ourselves. With regards to our fellow human beings, we need to love and accept them for who they are; accepting that everyone has a part to play in this life. What we have been gifted with is choice, we can put boundaries in place, we can keep people in our lives, we can limit the time we spend with them or we can walk away altogether; but expecting people to change so they can play life our way will cause all concerned a lot of pain and grind us down, as the life of others does not belong to us.

Always remember the importance of communication; talk to people! When going through hard times, faced with pain and difficult decisions, we tend to feel very alone, we believe no one can understand us, or what we are going through... and although technically this is true, as we each experience situations in our unique way in our own unique perspective, it is important to remember that other people can empathize, can relate, can support and can be there for us, with us, if we give them a chance; but more importantly if we give ourselves a chance, if we trust and let people in. I appreciate for many people is not easy, when I wrote A Reason to Love Me, and bared all to the world I was petrified! If you have read the book you'll know why, leaving myself open to judgement and criticism is an absolute contrast to my father's teaching and upbringing which are well encrypted within me. However, my purpose having grown bigger and stronger than my fear, fed my need to dare and lead by example; remind people that they are not alone, to let them know that it's okay to speak up, it's okay to reach out – that there is no shame - people will understand and relate so much more than we ever think is possible.

Since 'A Reason to Love Me' has been out, I have had a tirade of 'thank you' messages and other positive feedback. I said to my husband from the beginning if I could help even one person my mission would be accomplished, but I was not prepared for the response I got. Despite the 'severe nature' of some of its content, the response has been way above anything I was expecting, from people of different ages, gender and social backgrounds. People living in the same area as me for years, who had never gone beyond a "Hello", now telling me their life experiences, private, personal things they have kept to themselves, buried, for years in fear of judgement, of not being understood or being criticized. This shows, people really can relate. Bravery and courage come in many forms and in all sizes and that includes realizing that we don't have to face our problems, our fears, alone.

Do not allow the aggressors in your life to control you, always remember you have a choice. You can join them in persecuting you by pressing the replay button and staying stuck in those events, or you can stand up for yourself, build a better life in spite, and despite those events; breaking the chains and becoming the beacon of hope for others that need to find their way out of the dark. Don't meet them where they are, meet them where you are – in your peace, love and goodness. Your peace is too precious, don't throw it away just because someone is yet to learn what you already know.

Stop resisting and fighting against the current, be the creator of your life. Let go of the how things should be, learn to accept what was and dance with the how it is. You can focus on the 'should have's' or you can find the joy in your living; as I said, time will pass anyway, how you spend it and see it will determine a life of struggle or joy. You are the one in charge of the interpretation and energy you give to any situation. You are part of the puzzle in other people's lives, and in turn they are part of yours; all indispensable to complete each and every story.

I am a survivor of trauma, a variety of ones in fact. The opinions and techniques I have shared are those of my experiences and understandings whilst working through my healing. Whilst I do appreciate that my lessons are unique to me, I hope my writing and suggestions give you hope and intrigue you enough to give them a try, especially if you are in the process of healing yourself. I just want you to know that nothing is insurmountable, that there is always a way, a strategy, another path; and a change of perspective is often enough to help take our power back. As life really is now, and life is for living our way.

Life will give you love,
Will give you armor,
Will give you hope,
Will give you option…

Love, Live & Let Live – I dare you to open your heart and really READ and FEEL these words. Allow them to set you free.

Love, light and gratitude

Daniela x
Integrative Counsellor, Author & Speaker

About the Author

Daniela began her journey in rural Italy, surrounded by scrutiny and judgement, searching for love, acceptance and purpose. Her determination and hopes led her on a tumultuous journey that has seen her deal with the dramatic realities of her life. Using the strength and knowledge gained she has sought and found a balance and tranquillity she now channels into guiding and supporting others. Through her counselling and public speaking, she is now dedicated to helping others face and overcome their difficulties and demons in life and continues to deliver her message of love, hope and peace.

Printed in Poland
by Amazon Fulfillment
Poland Sp. z o.o., Wrocław